PROFESSIONAL SKILLS FOR COUNSELLORS

The *Professional Skills for Counsellors* series, edited by Colin Feltham, covers the practical, technical and professional skills and knowledge which trainee and practising counsellors need to improve their competence in key areas of therapeutic practice.

Titles in the series include:

Medical and Psychiatric Issues for Counsellors
Brian Daines, Linda Gask and Tim Usherwood

Personal and Professional Development for Counsellors
Paul Wilkins

Counselling by Telephone
Maxine Rosenfield

Time-Limited Counselling
Colin Feltham

Client Assessment
Stephen Palmer and Gladeana McMahon (eds)

Counselling, Psychotherapy and the Law
Peter Jenkins

Personal and Professional Development for Counsellors

Paul Wilkins

SAGE Publications
London • Thousand Oaks • New Delhi

SAGE Publications Ltd
6 Bonhill Street
London EC2A 4PU

SAGE Publications Inc.
2455 Teller Road
Thousand Oaks, California 91320

SAGE Publications India Pvt Ltd
32, M-Block Market
Greater Kailash – I
New Delhi 110 048

British Library Cataloguing in Publication data

A catalogue record for this book is available
from the British Library.

ISBN 0 8039 7462 0
ISBN 0 8039 7463 9 (pbk)

Library of Congress catalog card number 96-070927

Typeset by Mayhew Typesetting, Rhayader, Powys
Printed in Great Britain by Hartnolls Ltd, Bodmin, Cornwall

To my daughter Claire

Contents

Acknowledgements

I wish to acknowledge the efforts of all the people whose help and support I received in the writing of this book. In particular, my thanks go to my friend and colleague Barbara Douglas and the series editor Colin Feltham who both read and commented constructively on the manuscript in its various stages – this was invaluable. I am also indebted to all the friends and colleagues who spoke to me about their experiences of continuing development and who allowed me to use their words in this book.

1

What is Personal and Professional Development?

The commitment to personal and professional development is widespread in the world of counselling and psychotherapy. It is common to hear therapists of all kinds saying something like: 'You can only take a client as far as you have gone yourself.' Implicit in this statement is the belief that the development of the client is in some way limited by the development of the counsellor. Aveline puts it thus: 'What therapists can bear to hear in themselves, they can hear in their patients. What therapists can find in themselves, they can recognise in others' (Aveline, 1990: 333).

What isn't clear from such statements is to what reference is being made. Perhaps in the mind of many counsellors, the achievements are in terms of psychological insights and the reduction of emotional disturbance. It is true that a therapist with little self-awareness and who is emotionally ill-adjusted is unlikely to be effective with clients but perhaps other learning and insights are valuable to the client in the therapeutic encounter. It may be that we owe it to our clients to develop as human beings in some comprehensive way. Perhaps the extent to which we can facilitate the development of our clients is limited not only by our emotional development but (for instance) our cognitive, philosophical and ethical development. Personal and professional development may be about becoming a more complete practitioner but is also about becoming a fuller, more rounded person. Counsellors who belong to a professional organisation are professionally and ethically obliged to address their own growth and education in order to be better able to facilitate the growth of their clients. It could be argued that joining an appropriate professional association and/or engaging with peers in some other way is itself a stage in professional development. Increasingly there is an expectation that counsellors and other therapists will be members of such organisations and so offer their clients the protection this affords. Perhaps it is hard to conceive of a counsellor who practises outside this framework as working effectively or ethically.

Professional organisations recognise this obligation and include it in their codes of ethics and practice. Writing about continuing professional development (CPD) with respect to counselling psychology, James (1995a: 7) stated that 'CPD is a necessary component to being both an applied psychologist (Chartered Psychologist) and a Counselling Psychologist.'

Books on counselling and psychotherapy often make reference to the obligation for professional and personal development. Rowan (1976) writes of the responsibility of therapists to constantly address their own material (by which he means unresolved emotional issues and emotional reactions to the client) and Rogers entitled one of his principal works (in which he writes of his growth as a practitioner and as a human being) *On Becoming a Person* (Rogers, 1961). Palmer (1991) writing as managing editor of the BAC journal *Counselling*, compares 'continuing professional education' with supervision. He writes that not only do counsellors benefit from professional development but that clients may also benefit in the long run. Palmer regards continuing development and supervision as intrinsically linked and essential to good practice.

The notion that personal and professional development are vital to the proper functioning of a counsellor dates from the very earliest days of the profession. Freud was very clear that personal analysis was a necessary prerequisite for anyone wishing to become a psychoanalyst. In many approaches to therapy, this remains an essential principle. Many programmes of training require students to engage in personal therapy, usually with a therapist of the same orientation as that aspired to by the trainee. Even those programmes for which this is not a requirement (perhaps because of an awareness that counselling is essentially a consensual relationship between client and counsellor and that any hint of 'compulsion' is therefore contradictory) generally recommend that students engage in therapy. And, in my experience, personal therapy *does* seem to make a difference to the effectiveness of the trainee counsellor. As a counselling tutor, I have noticed repeatedly that my most successful students tend to be those who take constructive steps to address their personal issues *and* who have most practice with 'real' clients. It is as if these two elements (which I think correspond to elements of personal and professional development respectively) do more for the development of counsellors than any amount of class contact. I think that what is true for the trainee is just as true for the experienced and established practitioner – the amount of personal work we do and the amount of practice we get are primary factors in determining our effectiveness. It is equally true that, in some approaches to therapy (for instance the cognitive-behavioural approaches) personal therapy is seen as less important and so legitimately figures less in the developmental plans of the practitioners of these approaches. Additionally, it is important to realise that not all personal therapy is experienced as useful. There is research evidence to show that, sometimes, trainees have had unsatisfactory experiences of personal therapy. McLeod (1993: 198, 210–211) briefly reviews the evidence for the effectiveness (or lack of effectiveness) of personal therapy in the development of the trainee counsellor. He considers that there are 'reasons to expect personal therapy to be associated with greater counsellor competence, but also reasons to expect the reverse', and cites a number of research studies supporting one or other view. The whole area of personal therapy is explored more fully in Chapter 4.

It seems clear, therefore, that the importance of personal and professional development is widely recognised but what exactly is meant by these terms? Though codes of ethics and practice make reference to the necessity of these elements, they do not currently offer clear guidance as to what constitutes either professional development or personal development. It remains for individual practitioners to decide for themselves what these may be and then to set about discovering ways to meet the requirements of their professional bodies and to satisfy their personal needs. This is reasonable (each of us is unique, and our ways of growing and learning are different) but it is confusing. The commitment individual counsellors have to continuing professional development varies considerably. Some spend a great deal of time and money attending international conferences and others are offered the support of their employers. Some counsellors, for one reason or another, give professional development a low priority. Perhaps they are unsure of its importance, don't know how to go about the process or feel they can't afford the time, money and energy it takes. The purpose of this book is to enable practitioners to reach some personal understanding of their developmental needs and to suggest a programme through which these needs may be met and which is appropriate to their means.

Definitions

As in the title of this book, personal and professional development are usually bracketed together. This immediately raises the question – to what extent are they separate and to what extent are they indivisible? Perhaps there is no clear separation. From one perspective (that of therapists emphasising relationship above technique) counselling and other forms of therapy are most effective when the process involves a meeting of the real self of the therapist with the real self of the client. Satir (1987) states this most eloquently when she writes:

> Therapy is a deeply intimate state and vulnerable experience, requiring sensitivity to one's own state of being as well as to that of the other. It is a meeting of the deepest self of the therapist with the deepest self of the patient or client.

It is only when we pay attention to our own development that this 'intimate' state becomes possible for it is only then that we may fully appreciate its necessity *and* be confident that we may safely enter into it without losing ourselves. Only the personally strong can easily enter the vulnerable state of which Satir writes. The extent to which we can be vulnerable, open, aware of ourselves and the other is a product of our personal and professional development.

Alan Frankland, chair of the British Association for Counselling (BAC) individual accreditation group (personal communication, 1995) wrote: 'I take the view that in the context of counselling these [professional and personal development] are almost interchangeable since the professional work of a counsellor involves the use of self at all times', and, writing about the BAC scheme for individual accreditation (Frankland, 1995: 58):

> Since BAC adheres to a broad model of counselling and therapy which places the person and personal relationships at the heart of our work, there is no problem in subsuming personal development under professional development (and to some degree vice versa).

This reinforces the view that it may be fruitless to separate professional and personal development for the former is inextricably linked with our development as persons. This recognition seems to be international.

Smaroula Pandelis, a Greek therapist, wrote of her experience of attending a training conference (Pandelis, 1995: 9). At the start of this conference, she was issued with 'ethical guidelines for conference delegates' and she was struck by the statement that *the primary aim of the conference is training and education, not therapy*. Pandelis writes of the contradiction she perceived in this for, though she was fully aware that she wasn't at the conference to deal with her personal issues, at the same time 'on another dimension' she *was* there to work on her personal issues. She writes: 'I believe that my professional issues and my philosophical issues *are* my personal issues' (my emphasis).

Pandelis voices the contradiction or paradox that we face as counsellors when we try to determine our needs for personal development and our needs for professional development. They are indeed linked, mutually dependent and perhaps it is impossible to separate them. I am certain that, if they can be separated at all, the boundary is hazy and shifts with the moment. Perhaps rather than attempt to define them as two separate entities, the most useful approach is to view the continuing development of a counsellor as comprising a spectrum of elements. One end of the spectrum may be easier to define in terms of professional needs, the other as personal needs. As Skovholt and Ronnestad (1995: 1) report: 'the field has increasingly come to realise the intertwining of the personal and professional aspects of the functioning of the therapist/counsellor'.

The issue of continuing development is further complicated because both professional development needs and personal development needs change with time and experience and they are perceived differently by therapists of different orientations. It is likely that the needs of a beginning therapist and a practitioner of many years' standing will be quite different. Skovholt and Ronnestad (1995) describe an eight-stage model of the evolving professional self of counsellors and therapists. On the basis that

---

Box 1.1   Professional development includes:

- the updating of skills and knowledge by (for instance):
  - attending conferences
  - reading relevant journals
- formal training (including postgraduate work and specialist courses)
- developing a stance of 'reflective practitioner', that is of learning from experience
- engaging in the process of research

---

the boundary between the two may be somewhat fluid and that the most appropriate forms of professional and personal development change as therapists 'mature', I can offer definitions which I think are useful.

Professional development

The professional development of counsellors is that area which addresses the extension of skills and knowledge (see Box 1.1). It is the furtherance of ability as practitioner through (for instance) further training, professional updating and study of any kind. To meet this need, counsellors have a variety of means. Most professional organisations combine their AGM with a 'training conference' which offers not only keynote speakers addressing an issue of the moment but a variety of workshops from which an individual therapist may choose the most appropriate. Journals addressing the whole area of counselling and psychotherapy abound and offer the thoughts and conclusions not only of academics and practitioners but sometimes of students and clients too! Books on counselling continue to proliferate and offer insight into working with particular types of client, explanations of an approach to counselling in practice and the relevance of more general issues such as ethics, the law or the importance of cross-cultural issues.

The updating of skills and knowledge about counselling should be considered a professional obligation. Ideas and practices about how to work with particular clients, the role and nature of supervision and the effectiveness of particular techniques are constantly being revised. Classical approaches are increasingly being re-examined and re-developed and new techniques and strategies are emerging from research and experience. There is more and greater expertise across the whole field of counselling now than there ever has been. It is incumbent upon the conscientious practitioner to be informed of and take note of these changes even if they are not incorporated into practice. The journals and the events organised by the professional bodies provide an excellent way of keeping abreast of new ideas and changes in practice.

Formal training also provides an opportunity for professional development. There is a growing number of post-qualifying courses offering counsellors and other therapists the opportunity to study for a master's degree as well as a plethora of 'specialist' training. As well as traditional counselling courses perhaps with a psychodynamic, person centred or integrative orientation, there now exists the opportunity to train in psychosynthesis, multimodal therapy, cognitive analytic therapy, primal integration therapy, an abundance of creative approaches to therapy (such as art therapy, dance movement therapy or psychodrama) and a wealth of other approaches. There are also opportunities to extend professional skills beyond the field of client work through training as a supervisor.

Professional development though is not only about 'learning' in the sense of formal training and the study of somebody else's thought. It is also about reflection and discovery. I wrote above about how I had noticed that the amount of practice my students had affected their development as counsellors. This is because it is only as we work with clients that we understand more of our abilities and the relevance of our learning to practice. One way we develop as practitioners is to reflect upon our work and upon our clients. This reflection may take place in the formal setting of supervision, while making notes about the counselling session or as the result of listening to tapes of the counselling interaction but it is just as likely to happen in a less formal way. My personal favourites are musing in a warm bath or on a country walk. But it isn't where this reflection takes place that is important, simply that it does.

Discovery too is important to professional development. I often think that the whole process of counsellor training is really a journey of *discovery* rather than one of being taught, that is an uncovering of existing attitudes and skills, not a process of in-struction. Adherents of approaches based more on the acquisition and application of skills and techniques might take a different view, for their emphasis is (at least in some ways) on structured learning. Jenkins (1995: 203–206) discusses this difference in approaches to counsellor training. The former he refers to as an inductive approach (that is one emphasising process), seeing it as especially appropriate to, for example, person centred therapy or the psychodynamic approaches and the latter he says is a deduc-tive approach concerned with the acquisition of skills and tech-niques. Examples of approaches favouring a deductive approach to training are that of Egan and rational emotive behaviour therapy.

But discovery is arguably important to the development of the behaviour therapist and the cognitive behavioural therapist as well as to therapists of humanistic, psychodynamic or trans-personal leanings. Sometimes this discovery is through happen-stance but it can also be deliberate; that is as the result of research. This research could be of a highly structured nature and lead to a higher degree (at last, in the UK, there are growing numbers of counselling researchers and some university departments are very exciting places alive with new ideas) but it can just as easily be less structured, less formal and result from questions such as 'I wonder if . . .', 'What happens if . . .'. Most of us engage in research much of the time – but perhaps we call it satisfying our curiosity or even being nosy! Research and the deliberate development of a stance of 'reflective practitioner' are appropriate to all approaches to therapy and to all stages of the career of a therapist. Schon (1991: 49–50) maintains that the best professionals know more than they can put into words and that the 'spontaneous, intuitive performance of the actions of everyday life' demonstrates a special kind of knowledge. He goes on to write that practitioners 'often think about what they are doing, sometimes even while doing it'. Examples of the questions that practitioners ask themselves about their actions include:

- What features do I notice when I recognise this thing?
- What are the criteria by which I make this judgement?
- What procedures am I enacting when I perform this skill?
- How am I framing the problem that I'm trying to solve?

This contributes to the process of 'reflection in action' which, in the context of practice, is a powerful learning tool. Schon (1991: 61) writes:

> A practitioner's reflection can serve as a corrective to over-learning. Through reflection, he can surface and criticise the tacit understandings that have grown up around the repetitive experiences of a specialised practice, and can make new sense of the situations of uncertainty or uniqueness which he may allow himself to experience.

Research may lead to another legitimate area of professional development – the dissemination of the new knowledge, new thinking, new experience or new opinion. The dissemination may take many forms. The results of research or theoretical advances often appear as publications in journals or as books but other means are equally valid. Workshops provide an ideal way of passing on material best transmitted experientially, but contributions to the training of others or to a structured peer group discussion are equally valid.

Personal development

If professional development centres on skills and knowledge, then one way of considering personal development is that it embraces everything else which facilitates being a practising counsellor. This is a broad definition, perhaps so broad as to appear useless, but exactly what 'everything else' is will vary not only with the individual but over time. My personal growth needs and direction are not only different from anybody else's but also different from those I had a year ago and most certainly very different from those I had twelve years ago when I started my career as a counsellor. However, for all of us there are some common elements and common strategies which would fall into the area of personal growth.

Personal growth (as it is relevant to development as a therapist) is the process of attending to our own needs in such a way as to increase our ability to be with our clients in a way that is not only safe for both parties but which incrementally improves our effectiveness. It is about dealing with our blind spots and resistance so that we may better accompany our clients on their painful or challenging journeys rather than risk blocking them because they seek to enter areas which are frightening or painful for us. It is also about resourcing ourselves so that we have the energy and enthusiasm that effective work demands. Personal growth includes an obligation to address personal material which may inhibit our clients' therapy and also an equal obligation to care for the self of the therapist. If the self is the therapist's principal or only tool (which is true more for approaches emphasising the relationship between client and therapist than those in which technique is most important), then it is incumbent upon therapists to develop and maintain the self – that is to engage in the process of personal growth.

The routes to personal growth are legion: they vary with the philosophical and theoretical orientation and experience of the practitioner, they differ with respect to personal learning and life events too. What for one practitioner constitutes an effective path to self-development may seem nonsense to another. This may be less important than it seems. Perhaps what matters is an internal consistency: that is, the routes to growth practitioners adopt are in tune with their philosophy and practice. Our roads through life are as different as we are but perhaps there are some common means to growth?

Personal therapy is viewed by practitioners of many (but not all) schools as an effective or even necessary way of growing. For those taking this view, personal therapy provides:

- an opportunity to address personal material (which may be understood in terms of unresolved traumas, irrational beliefs, life scripts, conditions of worth, defence mechanisms or whatever other way is personally meaningful; this is clearly about personal growth);
- experience in the client role which aids the therapist's understanding of how *their* clients may be experiencing therapy;
- a learning opportunity. However subtly, as clients we are aware of how our therapist responds, what techniques are used. This awareness may very well inform our own practice and so is at least to some extent professional development;
- a way of stimulating natural creativity and spontaneity and the imagination and exploring a variety of issues;
- a means of identifying personal conflicts (unresolved issues or ingrained attitudes and prejudices) which practitioners may need to manage in their own practice.

Mearns (1994: 40) points out that it isn't necessary that counsellors successfully address *all* their personal issues in order to be effective. Some of the conflicts arising because of them *'can be made safe through awareness and management'* (italics added). That is, if counsellors are aware of personal issues which may colour their behaviour and act to minimise any effect this may have, then good, safe and effective practice is likely.

Mearns writes of his suspicion of counsellors who seek perfection through personal development. I share his preference for a therapist who is 'a trifle imperfect' but who knows of these imperfections and works with and within them. Letting go of this spurious quest for some sort of total adjustment or personal perfection is in itself a stage in personal development. Perhaps a 'fully functioning person' is one who accepts and even delights in idiosyncrasies even though they do not conform to some ideal? If this is correct, it is not licence for indulging in whimsy and eccentricity but a recognition of the value of individuality, an acceptance that we are all to some extent 'abnormal':

> Sometimes to function well, you just have to put your introspection aside and get on with living your life. (Di Grimshaw, dramatherapist and play therapist, personal communication, 1996)

Grimshaw recognises that her effectiveness as a therapist depends upon her completeness as a person and her ability to be fully present and engaged in the process of living. To do this she must sometimes lay aside the struggle for understanding and the tendency to become absorbed in *doing* to get on with the business of *being*. This process of being is of entering fully and acceptingly into the human condition, being a person and not just being a therapist. Of course, the net effect of this is that the person becomes a *better* therapist!

I think that one way my clients benefit in working with me is that they meet me 'warts and all'. I endeavour to be real in the encounter and I think my obvious lack of perfection, of benign all-seeing wisdom is actually empowering. Though the concept of congruence is seen as particularly important in the person centred approach, other approaches also recognise the benefit to the client of a lack of perfection in the therapist. For instance, from the psychodynamic approaches comes the concept of the 'good enough' therapist and the naive therapist. Jacobs (1988: 97–98) writes:

It is indeed through counsellors understanding themselves as ordinary human beings that they find relevant knowledge to apply to clients' situations. It is not a question of 'There, but for the grace of God, go I' as the counsellor listens to the client, but 'There am I too'.

As a counselling tutor too I have noticed the almost tangible relief that comes over my students when they realise that to be good counsellors they don't have to be free from personal difficulties and personal weaknesses. I notice too that they are much better practitioners after this realisation than they ever were before.

Personal therapy is only one way of facilitating development, for this is not merely the working through and/or identification of personal issues. Personal development is about a growing ability to enlist a rich variety of personal attributes freely and with discrimination in such a way as to bring a creative energy to the whole of life. Such a person thinks, feels, imagines, is creative, fallible, and self-accepting and is able to make their wholeness available in the therapeutic encounter. To do this fully, therapists need to have acceptance and understanding not only of themselves but also of other people and of the world around them. Personal development means increasing this acceptance and understanding and increasing the ability to use it. This is probably as (or more) likely to be facilitated by reading a good novel or watching a film as it is by an in-depth study of the latest research material, for it concerns extending knowledge of the human condition.

Personal growth also includes the responsibility that therapists have to maintain their fitness to practise. Of course this includes all the elements considered so far but it is also about being kind towards and considerate of the self. It is only by constantly refreshing and resting ourselves that we can maintain the emotional and spiritual fitness that is as essential to our profession as physical fitness is to the athlete.

Stages in personal and professional development

For each of us, developmental needs change with time. This may be to do with changing interests and professional interests or life events but it also relates to the natural course of evolution of the professional self. Although it is quite common for people to enter counselling and psychotherapy relatively late in life, a professional career may encompass thirty or forty years or even longer.

Box 1.2   The eight stages of Skovholt and Ronnestad

1. *Conventional stage*: the individual is untrained in counselling yet engaged in helping relationships.

2. *Transition to professional training stage*: the stage at which an individual makes a commitment to professional training and the first part of that training.

3. *Imitation of experts stage*: the stage of being an 'intermediate student in the field'.

4. *Conditional autonomy stage*: the new practitioner has entered a 'probationary' period, has clients but is 'under active supervision'. In this context, supervision has parallels with the relationship of a junior doctor to a consultant – it is not the same as the supervisory relationship common in British practice.

5. *Exploration stage*: the practitioner is now independent and has already accumulated a 'wide variety of professional and personal experiences' but is still meeting many new challenges.

6. *Integration stage*: the individual has been practising for a number of years after qualifying and brings a range of experience to that practice.

7. *Individuation stage*: individual paths of development have taken the practitioner in 'increasingly unique and separate ways'. Skovholt and Ronnestad say that individuation involves both separation and relatedness.

8. *Integrity stage*: practitioners at this stage of development have been in practice for many years (in this study, twenty-five to thirty-five years) and they make extensive use of experience rather than the theories of experts.

Freud and Rogers continued practising into their eighties and Ellis is still going strong, also in his eighties! It is unlikely that the developmental needs of a beginning therapist will be the same as those of a therapist with many years' experience. Skovholt and Ronnestad (1995) have studied counsellor development in relation to their eight-stage model of the evolving professional self (see Box 1.2). Their research is based upon interviews with 100 counsellors in Minnesota who ranged from volunteer beginners to senior practitioners.

For each of these stages, Skovholt and Ronnestad offer a definition, and describe:

- the central developmental task
- the predominant effect
- the sources of influence acting on the practitioner
- the role and working style of the practitioner
- the conceptual ideas used
- the learning process
- measures of effectiveness and satisfaction

The authors also consider the factors which decide whether a therapist develops or stagnates. They write that stagnation arises from

> the absence of continuous reflective experiences and the fending off from experiencing anxiety arising from confrontation with challenges and complexities which the therapist/counselor is not able to handle. (Skovholt and Ronnestad, 1995: 124)

The authors also warn against 'pseudo development' which is apparent development rooted in professional behaviour which 'results from the process of premature closure. Such behaviour is defensively motivated and predominantly repetitive' (ibid.).

Clarkson and Gilbert (1991: 143–144) use the term 'pseudo-competency' differently. For them, it is a state:

> where individuals may appear *objectively* to be able to do the task competently, but *subjectively* do not experience the confidence that they will be able to do it consistently well without severe anxiety and without strain or undue energy drainage afterwards.

Skovholt and Ronnestad (1995: 136) also write that the struggle with anxiety and feelings of incompetence which all their veteran counsellors described seems to be essential to achieving professional identity.

Although the work of these two authors relates most directly to the experience and conditions of therapists working in America, their findings are generally applicable to all therapists. In particular, it is important and relevant to pay attention to the evidence they offer that continuous reflection is the key to professional development and that, in its absence, however many courses they attend, practitioners risk entering into a state of pseudo development. It is pseudo development and stagnation which lead to decreased effectiveness and an increased likelihood of burnout. Developing as a counsellor involves struggle and the need to address different issues at different stages of a career. In the earlier stages, the developmental needs are perhaps for skills and knowledge (feelings of competence); in the middle stages development is about finding a way of being personally effective; and the developmental issues of the final stages of a professional career may include adjusting to the idea of retirement.

Personal and professional development as a requirement of professional bodies

The BAC, to which over 13,000 people in Britain belong and (if they practise as therapists) to whose codes of ethics and practice they subscribe, recognises the importance of personal and professional development to good practice. In the code of ethics and practice for counsellors (BAC, 1993), there is a number of references to these issues. The *Code of Ethics* refers to the obligation counsellors have to 'monitor and develop their own competence and to work within the limits of that competence'. In the code these issues are addressed in the section 'Issues of Responsibility' under the headings of 'Counsellor Competence' and 'To Self as Counsellor'. The latter includes the phrase:

[Counsellors] should maintain ongoing professional development

The BAC Accreditation Scheme includes as a criterion for individual accreditation that an applicant 'Gives evidence of serious commitment to ongoing professional and personal development such as regular participation in further training courses, study, personal therapy, etc.'

For other organisations to which therapists may belong these issues are equally significant. The Counselling Psychology division of the British Psychological Society (BPS) sees continuing professional development as important and its standing committee for professional affairs has it under active consideration. The BPS as a whole records that its divisions and groups 'have continued to raise awareness of the importance of CPD' (*Annual Report 1994–1995*). James (1995b: 5) writes:

Continuing Professional Development (CPD) is becoming a prominent issue for the BPS and Chartered Psychologists, as it is for other professional organisations. Counselling Psychologists should be familiar with the need to maintain standards of practice and develop expertise and knowledge once qualified.

Many of the constituent organisations of the United Kingdom Council for Psychotherapy (UKCP) also attach importance to personal and professional development. Some of them (for instance the British Psychodrama Association), like the BAC, include the obligation in their codes of practice.

Although professional organisations are clear that they recognise the importance of professional and personal development, there is less clarity about what they would recognise as satisfying the obligation the various codes lay upon individual members. This lack of clarity applies to both the nature of suitable professional and personal development and the quantity expected. Some other professional groups *do* demand a certain 'quantity' of professional development. For example, in England and Wales, teachers are required to participate in at least five days' in-service training (INSET) each year. Similarly, psychiatric nurses are expected to attend at least five study days in any three-year period. Other groups (such as social workers) have no professional obligation to continuing professional development.

The assessors for the BAC scheme for individual accreditation use the notion of 'input' and 'output', and they further subdivide these as 'passive' and 'active'. Frankland (personal communication, 1995) says that input consists of those activities which support and develop the counsellor. Passive input includes many of the elements I consider to comprise professional development such as attendance at courses and conferences and 'purposeful' reading, while more active input includes professional development such as undertaking a training workshop and personal therapy, which I consider to be personal development. Output embraces extensions of the counsellor's role perhaps through expanding an existing practice (which Frankland considers to be 'relatively passive') or developing a new course, becoming a supervisor or publishing. Most organisations would be in agreement with the elements of development recognised by the BAC and the division into passive and active elements is useful.

How much personal and professional development is 'enough'?

Like the BAC, it seems that most organisations take the position that it is perhaps less fruitful to quantify how much personal and professional development constitutes 'enough' and more appropriate to consider the ways in which individuals seek to meet these requirements and that they are *serious* in their intent A common view seems to be that what is necessary is that there should be evidence of development and that it makes sense and/ or that it has been processed in such a way as to be useful. Because of this, assessors for individual accreditation are likely to have different ideas of exactly what constitutes appropriate development. Some would see a life crisis successfully transcended as evidence of both personal and professional development; others would be better satisfied with content and dates of courses attended and evidence of engaging in personal therapy.

It seems to me that although this lack of precision could be bothersome, it actually works to the advantage of the individual counsellor for, rather than being prescriptive, it allows a personal route through these requirements. What professional organisations are seeking, it seems, is not so much the attainment of a list of targets but rather that practitioners are recognising their needs for continuing input and that they are rising to the challenge of making new outputs. Professional and personal development is about working in a sensible and coherent way to raise individual effectiveness. This means that any individual programme of development should ideally be balanced, comprehensive and compatible with the philosophy and practice of the therapist to whom it pertains. Humanistic or psychodynamic practitioners might be tempted to concentrate on emotional development but cognitive development is also likely to be relevant and appropriate; similarly, cognitive behavioural therapists are likely to have a need for emotional development. A good programme of development addresses all levels of professional and personal functioning. This is recognised by professional organisations, and practitioners are expected to be able to provide evidence of their efforts in this direction especially if they are asking to be considered for accreditation (BAC), chartering (BPS), registration (UKCP) or some other form of professional recognition. This evidence must be of a personally relevant programme sufficient to the needs of that particular practitioner.

It seems that it is the *quality* of continuing development which counts rather than its quantity. The impression I get from assessors for accreditation and members of committees addressing issues of practice and ethics is that they are less likely to be concerned with *what* or *how much* continuing development a practitioner has undertaken and more concerned with *how relevant and useful* this has been. Attending a three-day international conference may seem more impressive than reading a novel, but supposing the conference-goer paid scarce attention or found much of it irrelevant or uninteresting while the reader (who worked with abused young people) spent an hour or two with Alice Walker's *The Color Purple* and achieved more in terms of development? The resources devoted to development should be proportional to the amount and nature of the counsellor's practice. The development profile of a part-time voluntary counsellor could be very different from that of a counsellor employed full time. The art of undertaking 'enough' professional and personal development is to be able to explain convincingly why you did what you did, how you did it and how as a result of it your practice is different or you are different.

The monitoring and evaluation of personal and professional development

Whether the aim is professional registration or not, the responsibility for engaging in appropriate continuing professional development (which in this context includes personal development) falls on the individual counsellor. It is for each of us to decide what our needs and interests are and to set about meeting them in a relevant way and in such a manner that we could demonstrate our progress to another. Counsellors working in agency or institutional settings may need to incorporate the aims and strategies of their managers in a programme of development but the *responsibility* for continuing professional development remains with the individual.

An aggregation of odds and sods that sparkle having been put together magpie-like may have little substance and is unlikely to satisfy either the individual therapist or any accrediting body. What is required is something at least loosely structured and cohesive and behind which there is serious, demonstrable intent. It may very well be that this does mean that the practitioner will meet at least part of the need for development through attendance at a variety of short courses but there will be an aim to this and method in the way in which it is done. The task facing each of us is to shape and carry out a programme of development which we can monitor, evaluate and so continually update and refine. For some of us this may be a more or less formal process, perhaps with a clearly articulated plan; for others the process will be less formal and will include elements of spontaneity. Each attitude has its place and it may be most sensible to carry out professional and personal development in a manner which is consistent with the model of therapy the counsellor adheres to in practice and in response to the guidance of a supervisor, tutor or a group of peers. A practitioner of rational emotive behaviour therapy might construct, monitor and evaluate continuing professional development in a very different way from a person centred counsellor. What is essential is that there is purpose behind such a programme and that, through it, the practitioner is seeking not only to expand skills and address gaps but also to maintain a good standard of professional functioning by keeping 'healthy', resourced and continually refreshed.

Continuing professional development is about improving the service offered to clients (and employers) but it starts from the aims and interests of the practitioner. Initially this involves taking stock, asking questions about present abilities, present issues being encountered professionally and personally and present circumstances. This process may be one of personal reflection or it may be facilitated by discussion with colleagues and friends but it is also a proper subject to be raised with a supervisor, mentor or tutor. Some aspects may even be relevant to personal therapy.

Whatever means individual counsellors employ to decide upon their needs and how to meet them, it is incumbent upon them to monitor and evaluate the progression they make. Professional organisations rightly expect that mature, professional practitioners will be capable of reflecting upon their experience, training, strengths and weaknesses *and* that they will do so with purpose and to effect. To demonstrate this purpose and effectiveness, it is necessary not only to have identified professional and personal needs and to have decided on how they might be met but also to be able to show what progress has been made and how goals have been refined.

An example of this comes from the practice of 'Jane', an established and competent counsellor who had worked for some years in an institutional setting where she shared the cultural background of her clients. Jane took up a post as counsellor in a GP practice which included a large number of Asian patients. In her new job, Jane soon realised that her knowledge of the traditions and customs of her Asian clients was less than she had imagined. Jane decided that this limited her effectiveness as a counsellor and that it was something she wished to address. Jane's first recourse was to read about cross-cultural counselling and some of the issues it presented. This was useful but, for Jane, it raised more questions than it answered – for the first time she began to see how *her* cultural and racial background shaped and formed her philosophy. It was clear to Jane that in order for her to work in the way she wished, she would have to become more conscious of her own prejudices as well as of the customs and forms of expression of her new client group. The way to do this seemed to be to attend workshops addressing cross-cultural issues and in particular the role of a white counsellor with respect to a black client.

Jane did attend such workshops and found that she was able to address some of her personal issues and her own cultural stereotyping. The result has been that Jane feels more competent as a counsellor and has worked more effectively with her Asian clients.

Monitoring

In its simplest form, the monitoring of continuing professional development may comprise a diary in which achievements are recorded. Such a bare list (perhaps of courses attended or books read) is of limited use. It says nothing about *learning*, indicates little about *growth*. What is important to both the practitioner and any professional body is some indication of the *process* of learning. It is of less value to know which course was attended and of much greater value to know what happened to the practitioner as a result of attending that course. What was the reaction to the input? With what did the practitioner agree or disagree? How might the practitioner incorporate any new learning into practice? What goals does the practitioner have as a result of attending the course? The latter may include a desire to know more but may just as legitimately be never again to attend a course with similar content or the same trainer! Another effective way of monitoring development is through the keeping of professional and personal development logs. For some, these may be one and the same; others may wish to keep them separate. Keeping such logs is not universally useful and it does require time (but not necessarily a lot).

Professional development logs are a record of all the things a counsellor does which in some way inform practice. This may include any training undertaken, notes from supervision, anything striking occurring in practice and thoughts and ideas from any source which seem relevant to the professional function. A good professional log is much more than a list; it is a place in which the practitioner processes input and ideas. It will include reactions to formal input and supervision. This processing is a way of making input relevant to the experiences of the individual practitioner. The practitioner may very well relate new ideas to specific clients (though a professional log is about the practitioner keeping it and not another form of recording about clients).

Professional logs are not only about achievements and learning from others. When they are most effectively used, they will include a record of difficulties and ways in which the counsellor has been less successful. They are a forum in which the practitioner may reflect upon performance as well as learning. It is only through such reflection and processing that true advances are made.

A useful aid to this reflection may be the processing of tape recordings of sessions with clients. Rogers is often credited with the pioneering of the recording of therapeutic sessions and Thorne (1992: 247) writes of how important these early recordings were in the study of effective facilitative responses, the understanding of the therapeutic process and the training of therapists. This remains the case. Another useful tool in this context is Interpersonal Process Recall (IPR). This was developed by Kagan and his colleagues in the 1960s and is described in Kagan et al. (1963) and Kagan (1984). IPR is, in essence, a recall interview. Soon after the end of a recorded therapy session and in the presence of an interviewer, one of the participants watches or listens to the recording. At moments in the session which seem significant, the watcher pauses the tape and explores the thoughts and feelings he or she was experiencing in the original session. McLeod (1994: 147) writes:

> The distinctive merits of the IPR method are that it slows down the process of interaction, thus allowing informants to unfold more of their experience and awareness than they would normally be capable of disclosing, and that the skill and presence of the interviewer enables the informant to feel safe enough to be open in acknowledging all facets of the process.

Both audio-tape recordings and video recordings provide a wealth of material on which the therapist may reflect and which (if the issue of confidentiality has been successfully addressed) may be useful in supervision. The material and learning from such tapes undoubtedly find an appropriate place in the professional development log.

Personal development logs are similar to professional logs in that they are kept in order to monitor and provide a record of growth, change and areas of difficulty. The subject matter of a personal log is the thoughts, feelings and experiences of its keeper. Personal logs may be much more introspective and intimate than professional logs. Within these the practitioner may record speculation about blind spots, interactions with family and friends, feeling responses to outside stimuli (such as clients and their issues, films, novels, interpersonal interactions, etc.), doubts, fears and worries. They are a proper place for any issue that may be taken to therapy, and much more. Whereas the purpose of a professional log is principally to monitor learning and inform practice, a personal log is meant to enable personal growth. This may occur because through keeping it, a pattern of behaviour becomes apparent or a glimmer of a blind spot flickers into awareness. Such logs have, of themselves, a therapeutic function. The very act of writing may result in an unburdening or a flash of insight.

Evaluation

Any programme of development is useful only when it is evaluated. It is only as a result of evaluation that the effectiveness of the programme can be known and new goals formulated. Evaluation isn't necessarily a formal affair and it certainly isn't an alien or unusual process. We engage in evaluation when we emerge from a cinema and exchange views with a companion. Perhaps this interaction is confined to a simple statement about whether or not the film was enjoyable (or 'good', or 'bad') but as moments of the film are relived and reactions to them shared it may become a more complex process and may even result in a modification or change of view. The evaluation of personal and professional growth is similar. At the simplest level, evaluation comprises the comparison of a list of aims with a list of achievements. The closer the match, the 'better' the result. This is of limited use for it is not what new information has been acquired but to what use that information is being put that constitutes an evaluation of development. It is only through processing and personalising input that it ceases to be information and becomes knowledge. A proper evaluation will include not only a record of achievements in comparison with goals but also an indication of the effectiveness of learning, a statement of changes incorporated into practice and perhaps a statement of personal growth.

Professional and personal logs provide source material for such an evaluation. They are a record of development over time and (at their best) include speculation, processing and ideas. All of this is the meat of an evaluation because there is a clear indication of change (or lack of change) over time. Other sources of feedback also have a role in the evaluation of professional and personal development. Depending upon the arrangement a practitioner has, it is quite legitimate to seek the opinion of a supervisor. This is particularly relevant if a personal difficulty or skills gap has first become apparent through supervision. Course leaders and peers may also be a useful and appropriate source of feedback. In any case in which you are seeking feedback from another person, it is probably best to be quite specific in your request, to state what it is you want to know and why.

Whatever the process of evaluation, however formal and whether it is principally introspective or involves the active seeking out of feedback from others, it should be essentially constructive. If some goals have not been achieved it is much more useful to know why than to view this as 'failure'. Perhaps too many goals were set, perhaps some proved to be inappropriate or irrelevant, perhaps undeclared goals have been met instead, perhaps there are real difficulties to be addressed before a certain goal becomes attainable. An effective evaluation leaves the practitioner in a position to continue the process of personal and professional growth. It is the basis from which new goals are formulated.

Summary

Personal and professional development is about becoming a more complete practitioner and a fuller, more rounded person. It is for the benefit of the counsellor and also for the benefit of the client.

There are professional and ethical obligations on counsellors to continue their development. These obligations are stated in the codes of professional organisations.

Personal and professional development are (sometimes inseparable) elements of the process of continuing development.

Professional development comprises the extension of skills and knowledge through training, reading, reflection and research.

Personal development is the process of attending to counsellors' needs in such a way as to increase their ability to be with their clients. This may include personal therapy but does not entail a quest for 'perfection'. Physical and spiritual fitness are as important as emotional fitness. Needs for personal development change over time.

Developing as a counsellor involves struggle and the need to address different issues at different stages of a career.

Professional associations have requirements for personal and professional development. These are stated in codes of ethics and practice. These requirements and not expressed in terms of quantity.

The quality and relevance of professional development are seen as more important than its quantity.

To demonstrate professional and personal development, it is necessary to have identified professional and personal needs, to have decided how they might be met and to be able to show what progress has been made and how goals have been refined.

The keeping of personal and professional logs is an effective way of monitoring development. These logs provide source material for the process of evaluation.

2

Further Training

Training in counselling and therapy takes many forms. Some practising counsellors are the 'product' of courses recognised by the BAC and this guarantees a certain level of training and amount of class contact but many more have received their education in another (and not necessarily less valuable) way. Whether practitioners received their primary training on a college course leading to a certificate, diploma or master's degree, through a voluntary agency such as Relate or with one of the training organisations in the private sector, there are likely to be some things about that training which were good and some which were less good. For instance one of the courses at the University of Derby pays particular attention to the personal growth/personal development aspects of counsellor training, those at the University of the West of England address particularly the issues of culture, and the course at the Manchester Metropolitan University is known for the emphasis it places upon supervision. But just as the last of these is strong in supervision, so it may be seen as paying less attention to cross-cultural issues, for example. However good it may have been overall, every training in therapy leaves its graduates with gaps in their knowledge.

The way these gaps are experienced and the importance attached to them will vary with the individual. For example, practitioners who trained as person centred therapists but then decided that psychodynamic approaches hold more attraction will experience themselves as having greater gaps in their knowledge and skills than practitioners who are content with the orientation taught in their training courses. Some 'gaps' arise from the working conditions or interests of the individual practitioner: for a general training course to address them in sufficient detail may not be appropriate. For instance, most diploma level courses pay scant (if any) attention to counselling people considered to be mentally ill or who experience learning difficulties. There will also be some elements of which every practitioner should have some awareness that have been only meagrely covered in their training. However they have arisen, these gaps in training are a proper concern for continuing professional development and, arguably, have first priority in any programme of further training.

Making a change

Sometimes a practitioner wishes to make a change in philosophy and preferred mode of practice. Such a change is likely to be costly at least in terms of time and effort. There is a clear obligation on anybody who has received a training in one model and wishes to practise in another way to address that gap in knowledge and skills. The only satisfactory way of doing this is to retrain: some people would take the view that it is the only safe way. If you have trained as a person centred practitioner and wish to practise in a psychodynamic way (or vice versa), then you owe it to yourself and your clients to become fully acquainted with the philosophy and practices of your newly chosen orientation. Exactly what constitutes such a 'full acquaintance' is a matter for the conscience and judgement of the individual practitioner, although anyone applying for recognition, accreditation or chartering is likely to have to satisfy the assessors that they have adequate training and experience to practise in the way they profess. In this case, I see no alternative but to undertake substantial training (perhaps at a higher level) in which the practitioner would get a thorough grounding in the preferred theory and plenty of supervised practice. Short courses and background reading will rarely, if ever, offer sufficient input for such a switch, at least as far as the professional bodies are concerned. Even to arrive at an integrated approach drawing on one or more theories to evolve a philosophically consistent form of practice ideally involves a thorough understanding of those underlying theories. Garfield (1980), in a detailed study of an eclectic approach to psychotherapy, takes a different view. He considers that 'theory' may be relatively unimportant in the practice of therapy and points out that there is a difference between what people say and what they do. He says:

In my own experience, there have been rather frequent discrepancies between what therapists have said about a particular session in psychotherapy and what appeared to have taken place on the basis of a recording of the session. (Garfield, 1980: 2)

Garfield's emphasis is on therapist qualities and technique rather than on any theory of psychotherapy; that is, how psychotherapists are and not what they believe.

Retraining

Organised courses of professional training whether in the state or private sectors tend to be expensive, and funding for places is limited or non-existent. Any funding available is more likely to go to someone who is embarking on an initial training. Unless practitioners who wish to change (or add to) the skills and practices they acquired in their first training have benevolent employers or the personal means, a formal course of the traditional kind which would allow them to 'retrain' may not be an option. To some extent, this is recognised by training institutions, which are increasingly likely to offer courses on a modular basis and to allow the student to attend or undertake modules as and when they can afford the time and money but there is usually a restriction on the amount of time between registration for a programme of study and its completion. This may extend the availability of retraining but it still excludes those without the means to pay or who are unable to take time away from other responsibilities.

There is a long tradition of 'self-teaching' in the profession of counselling and psychotherapy. Most of the 'originators' were at least to some extent self-taught. Sometimes this arose out of dissatisfaction with their previous training or the realisation that another approach, a different philosophy, was more appropriate to them and the ways in which they saw human beings and the nature of human difficulties. Ellis, Berne, Rogers, Perls and Assagioli (to name but a few), because they found their original training inadequate or antipathetic to views they later formulated, could all be viewed as retraining by self-teaching. The profession as a whole accepts the validity of that training. This way of becoming a therapist dates back to the earliest days of the profession. With respect to their practice of psychotherapy, Freud and Skinner were largely self-taught. Although I think it may be fraught with difficulties, it is philosophically consistent with the traditions and development of psychotherapy and counselling that therapists retrain themselves.

While I advise caution in taking a 'self-teaching' approach, anyone contemplating such a course of action might like to consider the following programme of action:

1. Having decided upon exactly what the new orientation is to be, devise a programme of reading which will provide the background knowledge to support new practices. This reading should cover basic theory, philosophy, skills and practices and could profitably include accounts of practice written from the perspective of both practitioners and clients. Reading may also provide a guide to the criticisms of the new approach and recent developments in it. Such a programme involves the reading not only of introductory and classic texts but also accounts of research (most likely to be found in journals and conference proceedings).

2. Concurrently with the reading, it may be informative to see how the principles and theories of the new approach aid understanding of the processes in the counsellor, in their clients and between them and their clients. Similarly, the ideas and theories may be applied to people counsellors encounter in other areas of their life. Do these ideas 'explain' behaviour? Does the model of the person underlying the suggested practices fit people the counsellor knows? The objective is to reflect upon how the book-learning applies to 'real life'. At this stage, incorporating the new ideas into actual practice in a way that constitutes radical change may be unwise.

3. Once informed about the basic ideas of a new orientation and how they apply to people, it may be appropriate to experience the approach in practice. To do this, the 'trainee' has several options, and which is the most appropriate differs with the approach itself and the interests, means and needs of the therapist wishing to make the change. For some approaches, experience in the client role may be particularly appropriate and this certainly offers the opportunity for considerable learning. This is probably as true for the cognitive-behavioural approaches which do not traditionally emphasise the importance of personal therapy as for the humanistic and

psychodynamic approaches which do. An alternative or useful addition to this may be to attend one or more short courses or workshops where the new approach may be witnessed or experienced in action (for example the introductory short course in transactional analysis called TA 101). A third option is to attend the annual training conference of the professional group using the approach. This offers the opportunity to become acquainted with current thinking and perhaps to participate in workshops and seminars as well as to hear papers delivered.

4. Before incorporating the new learning into practice, it is advisable that the therapist discuss the change and its personal and professional implications with colleagues, friends and, most importantly, with a supervisor. If the therapist's current supervisor does not practise in the new way, it is probably desirable to change to a supervisor who does *and* who is willing to work with a novice. This is important because good supervision from a supervisor immersed in the approach and who is willing to pay special attention to the educational function of supervision is likely to prove an invaluable asset and to protect the therapist and the client from the effects of misunderstanding and/or misapplication of the new techniques.

Identifying and addressing gaps in training

If gaps exist in the initial training of all counsellors (and other therapists), how may they be identified and addressed? If the need for further training arises from work environment or from personal interest, then you may have a clear idea of what they are or at least where to start. Perhaps you are working with a client group the needs of whom were under-addressed in your training. This client group may share a human condition (for example, older people or people with learning difficulties), perhaps they are 'culturally different' or perhaps they share a problem or an issue (things that spring to mind are childhood sexual abuse, eating disorders, alcohol-related problems or being HIV positive). Your need may be for up-to-date knowledge about the client group and/or strategies for working with clients sharing the particular condition or issue. Less obvious or distinct development needs may also arise from the working environment. Many counsellors who work in institutional settings or have dual professional responsibilities (perhaps as nurses as well as counsellors) often experience tension and conflict between their own views and needs, those of their clients and those of the institution. The need for training here may be in conflict-management, the legal responsibilities of a counsellor or ethical issues.

To some extent, I agree with Merry (1994: 1) when he warns of the possibility of losing sight of the client and concentrating on the issue and so questions the proliferation of short courses, workshops and books addressing particular client 'problems'. Merry fears that an absorption on the part of the counsellor with issues of bereavement, sexual abuse or AIDS leads to a focus on 'the problem' not on the whole person of the client. This can be a real danger, but a case can be made that it is the issue the client presents which is important: it is for that reason the client is seeking help.

Actually, it is likely that *both* are important and that all of us are well advised to keep attention on the whole client, the relationship between client and therapist *and* the issues which the client says are important. I think it is legitimate to seek to address a shortfall in knowledge about an issue through reading or attending a workshop. In the USA, this may be seen as imperative because counsellors who ignore clinical indicators for particular conditions may be sued. It is important that practitioners deal with their own ignorance of and fears or ambivalence about a specific client group or perceived problem. It is important too that if you work with a particular group, you understand the language and the social norms of that group. Younger people, and people from ethnic minorities, for example, may behave and speak differently from the counsellor. These are things which are unlikely to have been addressed in a course of formal training, but information on them is widely available through short course input and from specialist books.

So far I've dealt with particular (and perhaps quite large) gaps. These have the advantage of being easy to spot and relatively easy, but perhaps costly, to address. It is the less obvious gaps – the gaps that were perhaps less obvious to trainers and so were not even identified or which result from issues that have arisen since the initial training of the practitioner – which are harder to identify. They may also be harder to address. There are not only gaps arising from how and where we choose to practise and which we incur through choices we have made, but also gaps which we are ethically and professionally obliged to address.

Cross-cultural issues in counselling

One of the most obvious of these gaps is that arising from a lack of education and experience with cross-cultural issues, including issues of gender, race, religion and class. The counselling profession has lagged behind other helping professions in the attention we pay to this group of issues. Lennox Thomas, being interviewed by Dupont-Joshua (1995: 181) reflected on this from his perspective as a black therapist:

> I felt that I couldn't actually practise as a psychotherapist and pretend that race wasn't an issue in psychotherapy. It was only in the course of my training that I realised how little colleagues considered issues of race in psychotherapy.

This is because we often assume that one of our principal values, that of acceptance, is all we need in order to address issues of race and culture (though I suspect that there may be deeper, culturally derived reasons too). There seems to be some sort of assumption that because we accept people for what and who they are and make every attempt to become aware of their perceptions or to enter their frame of reference we *are* addressing this problem. This is naive. Even in this assumption (of the merit of acceptance and 'understanding' from the point of view of another) we are possibly erring in terms of culture for we are attempting to impose values arising from Western intellectual tradition on people who may not subscribe to it and to whom it may make no sense. Lago and Thompson (1989: 207) offer an opposing view to that which states that the knowledge and skills of counselling are adequate for work with any client. They sum up this view thus:

(a) In order to understand relationships between black and white people today, a knowledge of the history between differing racial groups is required.

(b) Counsellors will also require an understanding of how contemporary society works in relation to race, the exercise of power, the effects of discrimination, stereotyping, how ideologies sabotage polities, and so on.

(c)　Counsellors require a personal awareness of where they stand in relation to these issues.

Cross-cultural issues in counselling are not only to do with acceptance (though perhaps each of us could fruitfully examine just how accepting we are of someone who is culturally different), but to do with differences in values and differences in experience. Dupont-Joshua (1994: 203) writes:

> Modes of communication, relating and concepts of emotional distress vary vastly between cultures . . . so practitioners need help to extend their perceptions of the counselling relationship.

To what extent can a white middle-class Briton truly understand the experience of being black British or black in Britain? If understanding is limited, how accepting is it possible to be? For many practising counsellors, this is likely to be a gap in their education and I suggest it is one we all have an obligation to address. Phung (1995: 62) writes movingly of his encounters with institutional racism, saying that 'White counsellors need to take on board the reality of racism experienced by their Black clients.'

Perhaps too we must own our complacency about these issues and realise that a lack of prejudice is not the same as cultural awareness. For those wishing to address this area, short courses are available (often facilitated or co-facilitated by black counsellors) and the BAC has published a list of references to counselling, culture and race (Lago, 1995: 31–32). Lago says that 'Detailed knowledge is required of these phenomena (race and culture) before combining them with the activity of counselling' (ibid.: 31).

The experience of counsellors who attend courses dealing with cross-cultural issues is often revelatory. After participating in such a course, Jackie Bullows (personal communication, 1995), a counsellor working with people who have problems related to the consumption of alcohol and in primary health care, spoke of her amazement at her ignorance of black culture and black history. She was particularly struck because although throughout her whole working life she had encountered people from different races and cultures and regarded herself as relatively accepting of people, it wasn't until she made a conscious effort to examine her own values and to encounter those of black people that she truly appreciated the significance of such a process. Jackie's view is that this is an essential aspect of the continuing development of

---

Box 2.1   Suggested reading: race and culture

BACKGROUND READING

Fryer, P. (1984) *Staying Power: The History of Black People in Britain*. London: Pluto.

Pedersen, P. (ed.) (1985) *Handbook of Cross-Cultural Counselling and Therapy*. New York: Praeger.

Sue, D.W. (1981) *Counselling the Culturally Different. Theory and Practice*. New York and Chichester: Wiley.

Terkel, S. (1992) *Race*. London: Sinclair-Stevenson.

TRANSCULTURAL THERAPY IN PRACTICE

D'Ardenne, P. and Mahtani, A. (1989) *Transcultural Counselling in Action*. London: Sage.

Eleftheriadou, Z. (1994) *Transcultural Counselling*. London: Central Book Publishing.

Lago, C.O. and Thompson, J. (1996) *Race, Culture and Counselling*. Buckingham: Open University Press.

Kareem, J. and Littlewood, R. (1992) *Inter-cultural Therapy: Themes, Interpretations and Practice*. Oxford: Blackwell.

---

counsellors and that it isn't until these issues are faced that we realise the extent of our ignorance and the importance of addressing it. Therapists wishing to begin an investigation of issues of race and culture may find the selection of suggested reading in Box 2.1 useful.

Race is an important issue. Other cultural differences counsellors may need to address include those of gender, sexual orientation, disability and class.

Counsellors and the law

B.2.6.1 Counsellors should work within the law.

B.2.6.2 Counsellors should take all reasonable steps to be aware of current legislation affecting the work of the counsellor. A counsellor's ignorance of the law is no defence against legal liability or penalty. (BAC, 1993)

A second area of ignorance for many of us seems to be that connected with the practice of counselling and the law. We tend to be aware of our ethical obligations and our professional obligations, for these are values arising from our theory and practice and raised on courses and through the professional organisations, but to what extent do we know our legal obligations? Jenkins (1992: 165–167; 1996) has written about the possible functions of law in relation to counselling. He considers some of the benefits which would 'accrue from considering counselling in relation to the law' to be:

- setting counselling within a wider social frame
- specifying the nature of counsellor liability
- clarifying boundaries for counsellor/client behaviour
- denoting clients' rights

As yet, no British therapist has been prosecuted for professional misconduct or negligence but there are indications that it is just a matter of time. The furore about 'false memory syndrome' indicates that at least some people are open to the notion that we may use our professional skills to further our own ends, to convince clients that something happened to them because it suits our theories or our needs. This, in itself, indicates the possibility (and some would argue probability) of prosecution. The views and work of Masson (1992) in his critique of therapy indicate the abusive potential in the role of therapist. There are support networks (for example POPAN) for clients who have been abused by their therapist and the press and television have addressed this issue on more than one occasion. Already, we are beginning to behave defensively. Many BAC members and members of related organisations now take out professional indemnity insurance. Some organisations even make such cover a professional obligation.

It seems that not only do we not always understand our liabilities with respect to our clients but that we do not understand our responsibilities under the law. For instance, counsellors as a group seem confused about issues such as suicide, the expressed intent of a client to commit a crime and sexual, physical and emotional abuse of or by a third party. We may have a view arising from personal morality and, rather dangerously, assume that our view accords with the law, but how many of us are actually clear about legal obligations and the consequences of not following them through? This neglected area is now beginning to be addressed both on some courses and through new publications. Bond (1993: 232) lists the following statutes (see Box 2.2) as relating to the practice of therapy.

Box 2.2 Statutes relating to the practice of therapy

- Access to Health Records Act 1990
- Access to Personal Files Act 1987
- Children Act 1989
- Coroner's Court Act 1988
- Criminal Law Act 1977
- Data Protection Act 1984
- Education Act 1944
- Further and Higher Education Act 1992
- Human Fertilisation and Embryology Act 1990
- Mental Health Act 1983
- Police and Criminal Evidence Act 1984
- Prevention of Terrorism (Temporary Provisions) Act 1989
- Suicide Act 1961

Bond (ibid.: 38–39) advises that the law will change on significant points. He says it is important that, in the case of need, up-to-date professional advice is sought. The practice of counselling and psychotherapy may also impinge upon other areas where knowledge of the law is important.

Issues of mental health are governed by the Mental Health Act 1983 (and revisions to it in 1995). Indeed, medical and psychiatric issues in general relate to the practice of counselling. This is especially true for therapists working in primary health care or psychiatric settings but perhaps as a profession we need to raise our 'psychiatric awareness'. Daines, Gask and Usherwood (1996) have written on these issues.

Anyone whose practice involves work with children and young people or on issues relating to their well-being may need to know of the provisions of the Children Act 1989. Jenkins (1993: 274–276) has written about the position of counselling and counsellors with respect to the Children Act. He points out that the Act makes several references to the activity of counselling. Jenkins (1996) takes this exploration further.

Other major issues

I have separated cross-cultural issues and the law from other issues since they are important to the profession as a whole because they are to do with the context in which therapy occurs. They are issues which do (or at least should) concern us all. Other

---

Box 2.3   Questions to ask when assessing developmental needs

- For what did my original training equip me?
- What have I learned since?
- What issues do my current clients present?
- To what extent do the first two match the third?
- What do I want to know more about?
- What types of clients/client issues do I *not* encounter in my practice?
- What new developments are there in counselling and psychotherapy?
- What do my supervisor and my colleagues tell me about my abilities?
- What do I find most difficult in my practice?
- What would I like to be different about me and my practice in two (five, ten) years' time?

---

gaps tend to be more personal, specific to an individual's needs and interests though perhaps no less important.

Because they are more personal, to address these gaps is an individual task. It is a worthwhile task for every therapist to reflect upon their training and their experience. Together with some awareness of current issues in the theory and practice of counselling (perhaps gathered from journals or attendance at workshops and conferences) and a consideration of the issues being encountered in daily practice, this provides a basis for determining gaps in knowledge and practical ability. Because it is in the nature of blind spots that they are extremely difficult for the person who has them to perceive, this process of reflection is most easily performed with one or more colleagues. It may be a task for supervision or conducted with a group of peers.

Perhaps the easiest way to assess current knowledge and current practice (and therefore developmental needs) is to systematically pose and answer a number of questions (see Box 2.3).

This list is by no means exhaustive, nor is it prescriptive, but to use something like it as a basis to determine needs is likely to be helpful. Any other way of discovering what is known (questions 1 and 2) and how that relates to current practice (questions 3 and 4) together with what is exciting and interesting (question 5), what may be missing (questions 6, 7 and 8) and what ambitions and plans the therapist has (question 10) will provide a useful indication from which a plan for addressing gaps in training may be drawn. Dryden and Feltham (1994a: 119–122) offer a list of questions therapists may pose to themselves in order to establish their 'counsellor profile'. These questions address areas of skills, theoretical understanding, views of clients and their concerns, competence and the evaluation of practice. This too would form a useful basis from which to determine training and development needs.

Going further

Most counsellor training programmes in Britain are offered at the level of diploma or postgraduate diploma although an increasing number of courses for prospective practitioners are offered at master's level and a few lead to a certificate. Whatever they are called, these programmes are designed to take the student beyond the practice of counselling skills into the theory and practice of counselling *per se*. They normally include an in-depth study of one particular approach to therapy, a consideration of process in the therapeutic relationship and require students to be in supervised counselling practice. The intention of the tutors of these courses is to provide students with the experiences and opportunities which will allow them to become counselling practitioners. There are (and certainly have been) other routes to this status. This is clear from the routes to accreditation offered by the BAC.

However the individual has arrived at the level of training and expertise sufficient for them to recognise themselves (and be recognised by relevant professional organisations and their peers) as counselling practitioners, there exist opportunities to take the academic study of counselling and therapy further. There are now a number of courses at master's level which offer counselling practitioners the opportunity to reflect upon and develop practice. These are taught courses with the requirement to produce a dissertation, but for some at least this dissertation need not be a traditional 'research' topic but may comprise a reflection on practice, an in-depth case study or series of case studies. Generally speaking, the aim of these post-qualifying courses is to provide the student with the opportunity to build on and expand existing skills and knowledge. They may be based on a particular core model and will almost certainly reflect the interests of the staff groups offering them but they may also offer each student the opportunity to select personally relevant elements from a 'menu'. It is only by a thorough inspection of the information produced about any course and (perhaps) through dialogue with the tutors that the suitability of it to the prospective student's needs may be determined. Courses of this nature may include elements on supervision, current issues in counselling practice and (because of the dissertation element) input on relevant research methods. They may also include an opportunity to study the more 'exotic', such as creative approaches to therapy.

Courses are advertised in the postgraduate prospectuses of the institutions offering them and sometimes in therapy journals (especially *Counselling*) and the national press. They are usually part time and may very well be offered with a 'non-traditional' mode of attendance. Rather than college attendance for one day a week, for example, these courses may comprise block or occasionally weekend attendance with some portion as distance learning. Course teams tend to be very conscious of the time commitments of prospective students.

In addition to taught master's level courses (and the PhD in qualitative research in counselling and psychotherapy at Regent's College, London which has a taught element), there are numerous opportunities for suitably qualified candidates to pursue a higher degree by research. Such research studies may lead to an MA, MPhil or PhD depending upon the extent of the study and may be either full time or part time. Research degrees do not have the attendance requirements common in taught programmes and to this extent may be an easier opportunity for a practising counsellor. In other ways research degrees may be very consuming of time, energy and (especially in the middle stages) of enthusiasm. For this reason the decision to embark on such a course of study shouldn't be taken lightly. A prospective research student is well advised to approach potential supervisors at a very early stage. This is not only to check out the feasibility of the proposed research but to determine whether the required nature and level of support are available from the supervisor or team of supervisors. The issue of compatibility may be as important as the issue of relevant expertise and knowledge.

Most university departments offering the opportunity to study counselling at postgraduate level (and some that don't) will be prepared to consider applications from potential research

---

Box 2.4   Things to consider before starting postgraduate work

- Can I/ do I want to engage in a long and sometimes lonely process of research?
- What is my area of interest? What is it I want to know more about?
- What (if anything) is already known about this and who knows it best?
- How much time, energy, intellectual ability and money can I put into this investigation?
- What institutions in which I am interested may be able to offer me the support I need?
- Who in that institution has an area of interest close enough to mine to be able to act as a research supervisor?
- Can I work with that person?
- Is the library adequate to my potential needs?
- Will there be an adequate facility for processing the data I collect (both in terms of expertise and equipment)?
- Are there other researchers with whom to share ideas and for mutual support?
- Does the supervisor/institution have a good track record for the successful completion of research degrees?

---

students. Besides cost and geography, there are several other issues affecting choice of institution and supervisor, and the potential student might like to find the answers to a number of questions (see Box 2.4).

It is not essential that *all* these queries receive perfectly satisfactory answers, though I think that those of motivation and potentiality *do* require strong, affirming answers. It may be desirable to have the support of other research students but any lack here may be compensated for elsewhere. A proven track record may indicate that high quality support is available but someone new to academic supervision or with few students may offer more individual attention. What is important is that a potential student is relatively well informed about the prospects of a successful completion of the programme of research under consideration. These include the ability and motivation of the student, the feasibility of the investigation itself (is it really suitable to the level of study proposed?) and the resources of the institution and the proposed supervisor or supervisory team. If all of these exist then, with the assistance of the supervisor, the student has every possibility of putting together a viable research proposal and pursuing that research to the desired end.

As well as post-qualifying master's programmes and research degrees, there are a number of 'specialist' training courses at master's level. These differ from the former in that though they accept people with training and experience as therapists, they are actually a training in *practice*. In a sense, they are 'first level' courses. These are suitable options for counsellors who wish to develop as practitioners of a different orientation (they include, for instance an MA in Gestalt therapy at the University of Derby and an MA in existential psychotherapy at Regent's College) and perhaps to those who seek training as a 'psycho-therapist'. These courses involve the student in not only academic study but also supervised practice in the model forming the theoretical core of the course. They may also require that the student is in personal therapy with a therapist practising in that approach. These courses are offered on a part-time basis (occasionally full-time), sometimes in association with another institution.

Some therapists who are qualified as 'counsellors' may be tempted to undertake a course of training leading to a qualification in 'psychotherapy' assuming that the latter is in some way different from and 'deeper' than the former. This may be so and certainly makes more sense for practitioners of some orientations than those of others.

The issue of the difference between psychotherapy and counselling has given rise to a perennial debate. Naylor-Smith (1994: 284–286) is sure that (for psychodynamic approaches at least) there *is* a difference. He sees this difference as relating to the nature and frequency of the work done with clients and (by implication) the training of the therapist. Thorne (1992: 244–248) on the other hand is equally sure that the quest for difference is spurious. Woolfe, Dryden and Charles-Edwards (1989: 7–8) list some of the points made by people who see a difference between the two but offer the opinion that 'attempts to resolve this issue in terms of some over-reaching theoretical plan are futile and serve no purpose'. It seems to me too that this debate is irreconcilable. People are arguing from different definitions (which often arise out of different philosophies) and/or circular definitions: that is, 'Psychotherapy is different from (or the same as) counselling because I define it so.'

This issue is further complicated because some training organisations (such as Regent's College and the University of Leicester) offer courses with both 'counselling' and 'psychotherapy' in the title. Others (such as the Institute of Psychosynthesis) offer a qualification in counselling which may be converted to a qualification in psychotherapy by a further period of training (perhaps one year) and more practice.

The differences between the experience, competence and ability of people who consider themselves to be counsellors and those who bear the label 'psychotherapist' may be less than are imagined. As a registered psychotherapist, I have participated in over 1,500 hours of training (the BAC asks for 450 hours in a recognised course) but I am under no illusions that this in itself guarantees any greater knowledge or competence than that of graduates of the course in counselling practice with which I am associated as a tutor. Counsellors often do similar work with similar clients to the work done by therapists bearing the designation 'psychotherapist'. This isn't always appreciated by members of either group.

Practitioners attending a workshop on issues of race and culture in counselling became involved in a debate about the relevance of the input for a small group who identified themselves as psychotherapists and as therefore having different needs from most of the participants who called themselves counsellors. By lunchtime, when all the participants had been asked to reflect upon these issues with respect to their own practice and their own clients, both groups had become certain that little, if anything, separated them. This should be borne in mind by anyone seeking further training, as should the fact that the title psychotherapist is currently seen by many as 'user unfriendly'. Psychotherapists working in primary health care find they get more clients if they call themselves counsellors.

I do not mean that counsellors should never seek a further qualification which would be described as a qualification in psychotherapy. This is a route I have taken myself. I do think though that anyone considering a further qualification should look very carefully at the content and practice requirement of any course in psychotherapy to see how it compares with their original qualification. It may be that their knowledge and experience already place them far in advance of the abilities of new graduates of such courses. In short, it is the content of a course and the enthusiasm of the student, the desire to learn from the opportunities offered by the course, which are more important than its title.

Something different

For many counsellors their perceived training need is not the pursuit of a higher degree, whether or not by research. What is more attractive and relevant is the expansion of skills into another area. There are many types of therapeutic endeavour not usually covered in conventional training courses but for which training at various levels is available. These include training in the area of creative therapies such as psychodrama, art therapy, dance movement therapy, transpersonal therapies such as psychosynthesis and many others. Even a brief look at the book on 'innovative' therapies edited by Rowan and Dryden (1988) will give some indication of the range of possibilities, and their list is by no means complete – indeed it is one to which additions are constantly made. Feltham (personal communication, 1995) in an attempt to give 'a flavour of the current range and proliferation of psychotherapies' offers the list in Box 2.5.

Some of these other ways of being a therapist are offered as full trainings in their own right: that is they assume that the would-be practitioner is starting from scratch. Many of them are offered in the private sector rather than through the educational institutions provided by the state. Such trainings include those in person centred expressive therapy, psychosynthesis and (most) psychodrama. On the other hand, most training in drama therapy, art therapy and dance movement therapy is now available through colleges in the state sector. Some of these different approaches are, in a sense, 'conversion courses' aimed at increasing the skills of people already in practice as therapists. Cognitive analytic therapy (CAT) seems to fall into this category.

Short courses and workshops

For most practitioners, short courses and workshops provide an excellent way of satisfying the 'ongoing training' element of continuing professional development. These may address theory or practice and may be taught, experiential or offered in a way which combines both formal teaching and a chance to experience

---

Box 2.5 Different therapeutic orientations

Adlerian Therapy
Art Therapy
Behaviour Therapy
Biodynamics
Bioenergetics
Biofeedback
Biosynthesis
Body Psychotherapy
Clinical Theology
Cognitive-Analytic Therapy
Cognitive Behavioural Therapy
Cognitive-Interpersonal Therapy
Cognitive Therapy
Communicative Therapy
Contextual Modular Therapy
Daseinanalysis
Dialogical Psychotherapy
Dramatherapy
Encounter
Existential Therapy
Experiential Psychotherapy
Feminist Therapy
Focused Expressive Therapy
Focusing
Gestalt Therapy
Hypnotherapy
Implosive Therapy
Inner Child Advocacy
Integrative Psychotherapy
Intensive Short-Term Dynamic
    Psychotherapy
Jungian Analysis
Kleinian Analysis
Lacanian Analysis
Lifeskills Training
Logotherapy

Micropsychoanalysis
Morita Therapy
Motivational Interviewing
Multimodal Therapy
Narrative-Constructivist
    Therapy
Neuro-Linguistic Programming
Object Relations Therapy
Past Lives Therapy
Personal Construct Therapy
Person Centred Therapy
Primal Integration
Process-Oriented Psychotherapy
Psychoanalysis
Psychoanalytically Oriented
    Psychotherapy
Psychodrama
Psychosynthesis
Rational Emotive Behaviour
    Therapy
Reality Therapy
Rebirthing
Redecision Therapy
Re-evaluation Counselling
Reichian Therapy
Rolfing
Sex Therapy
Single-Session Therapy
Social Therapy
Solution-Focused Brief Therapy
Stress Inoculation Training
Systematic Therapy
Transactional Analysis
Transpersonal Therapy
Twelve Steps Therapy
Will Therapy

---

techniques or skills. They are usually designed to introduce participants to an area of counselling with which they may not be familiar or to provide an updating of skills in the light of new knowledge. Although there is some confusion or overlap in the terminology (one organisation's workshop is another organisation's short course) workshops are generally of relatively short duration (hours rather than days) and short courses are somewhat longer. For example, workshops at Sheffield Hallam University last for one or two days and short courses for 30 hours.

Short courses and workshops are offered by many organisations and vary greatly in cost. They include training sessions offered by local branches of the BAC (which usually last only an hour or two as part of a regular branch meeting), workshops offered in conjunction with established training courses in both the private and public sectors as well as those which stand by themselves. The cost of a course is a product of its length, the number of participants and the needs of the provider. As a general rule, courses offered by institutions in the public sector are likely to be cheaper than those offered by private institutions and independent trainers.

Short courses offer established practitioners a focused way of fulfilling their needs for further training. Such needs are usually based on a desire to update knowledge in a quite specific area (such as issues of race and culture or working with adults who have been sexually abused as children), or to sample a different set of skills or way of working. Short courses also provide a way of sampling an approach before making the commitment to lengthy training. A subsidiary need may be to address any shortfall of training hours necessary for professional accreditation.

How to find out about short courses
Some short courses are advertised nationally (for instance in the counselling press, including *Counselling* and *Counselling News*) or regionally in 'what's on' magazines like *Caboots* in the northwest and *Time Out* in London, but many are not. Short courses tend to be provided with the expectation that attendance will be by members of the local counselling community. Unless you are well attached to the local grapevine, the chances are that many short courses will pass you by unnoticed. Finding out what these are and where and when they are offered may present quite a challenge! Providers of short courses tend to advertise them to people they already know or through specialist publications. One way to find out what is going on is to make sure that you are included on the mailing lists of likely providers of courses and/or discover where therapy courses in your area are likely to be advertised. Local libraries tend to be a good source of information about local events.

Local associations of therapists often organise workshops and other training events. In the north-west for instance, the local branch of the BAC provides input covering a wide range of counselling-related topics, Dramatherapy North West has a series of one-day workshops and a summer school, and North West Psychodrama also organises workshops in the area. Universities and colleges which provide a training in counselling may offer workshops which (for a fee) are open to the public. In Manchester both the University of Manchester and the Manchester Metropolitan University offer workshops on some weekends, and between them offer training relevant to many areas of therapeutic endeavour. Similarly, City College, Manchester offers an open Easter school in conjunction with its diploma in dramatherapy. The NHS, charitable institutions and private institutions also all offer short courses in the broad field of counselling and therapy. In Manchester the NHS provision includes a training in creative approaches to group therapy, the NSPCC offers training in psychodrama and private institutions such as the Gestalt centre offer a variety of short courses dealing with their own approaches to therapy. This pattern is, I believe, typical of most big cities. In York, for instance, there are summer schools focusing on the ideas and approach of Gerard Egan and dramatherapy. Short courses are by no means confined to cities and other centres of high population. Many professional organisations hold annual training conferences or summer schools which tend to be held in a different part of the country each year. As well as being for members of the organisation, these are commonly open to non-members.

Reading

Experiential work, reflecting on practice, doing research and exchanging views and opinions with colleagues are all valuable ways of continuing learning but perhaps reading is one of the principal means by which practitioners may extend their knowledge. Books and journals are widely available and (sometimes with some effort) may be borrowed rather than bought. Academic libraries, especially at institutions where counselling, psychotherapy or psychology are taught, tend to stock a wide range of books and journals relevant to therapy. Public libraries are much more restricted in the choice they offer but all libraries may make use of the inter-library loan scheme through which any book and any paper are available to any reader. One of the peculiarities of the most frequently used library classification systems is that it has no shelf-mark for counselling *per se*. Books on counselling may be classified as psychology, psychotherapy, social work or even education and these groupings are not usually found close together on the library shelves; which book is shelved where seems to be a result of the librarian's preference. This makes casual browsing difficult. Visits to the library may be less frustrating if you have a good idea of what you are looking for!

As books on counselling and psychotherapy continue to proliferate, practitioners are faced with the problem of deciding what to read and how to get hold of the material. Reviews in journals may provide a useful guide to new publications (but not all books are reviewed and it is possible to form an opinion different from that of the reviewer) but many older books are still well worth reading. For most approaches to therapy, there are what might be considered 'classic texts' (some of these are given in Box 2.6) and these with, for example, books in the two series 'Counselling in Action' and 'Key Figures in Counselling and Psychotherapy' published by Sage can form an ideal introduction to an orientation, theory or mode of practice.

For any practitioner, keeping up with the literature can be a problem – not only is there so much of it but it isn't always easy to know just what has been published. For practitioners with access to a large bookshop, browsing the relevant shelves may be helpful, but not even there do all titles appear. Publishers of books relating to the theory and practice of therapy regularly issue catalogues of their books in print – these catalogues often address 'specialist' areas and books of interest to counsellors and other therapists are likely to be found in those addressing social science or psychology. Publishers may be happy to supply prospective purchasers with these catalogues. A list of some of the major British publishers producing books on counselling and psychotherapy is given in Box 2.7.

When from a review, a catalogue or by word of mouth you discover a book you wish to read, there remains the problem of access. If you wish to borrow rather than purchase then the largest library to which you have access is your best resort. This library (perhaps for a fee) will be able to secure for you a copy of any book published in English – but be warned: this might take a

---

Box 2.6   A selection of classic counselling texts

COGNITIVE-BEHAVIOURAL APPROACHES

Beck, A. (1976) *Cognitive Therapy and the Emotional Disorders*. New York: New American Library.

Ellis, A. (1962) *Reason and Emotion in Psychotherapy*. New York: Lyle Stuart.

HUMANISTIC APPROACHES

Berne, E. (1961) *Transactional Analysis in Psychotherapy*. New York: Grove Press.

Berne, E. (1975) *What Do You Say After You Say Hello? The Psychology of Human Destiny*. London: Corgi.

Perls, F.S. (1969) *Gestalt Therapy Verbatim*. Lafayette, CA: Real People Press.

Perls, F.S., Hefferline, R.F. and Goodman, P. (1951) *Gestalt Therapy: Excitement and Growth in the Human Personality*. New York: Julian Press.

Rogers, C.R. (1951) *Client-Centred Therapy: Its Current Practice, Implications and Theory*. London: Constable.

Rogers, C.R. (1961) *On Becoming a Person*. London: Constable.

INTEGRATIVE APPROACHES

Egan, G. (1986) *The Skilled Helper: A Systematic Approach to Effective Helping* (3rd edn). Belmont, CA: Brooks/Cole.

Lazarus, A.A. (1981) *The Practice of Multimodal Therapy*. New York: McGraw-Hill.

PSYCHODYNAMIC APPROACHES

Bowlby, J. (1969) *Attachment*. London: Hogarth Press.

Erikson, E. (1950) *Childhood and Society*. New York: W.W. Norton.

Freud, S. (1949) *An Outline of Psychoanalysis*. London: Hogarth Press. (See also the Pelican Freud Library published in several volumes by Penguin.)

Jung, C.G. (1963) *Memories, Dreams, Reflections*, ed. A. Jaffe. New York: Pantheon.

Klein, M. (1975) *The Writings of Melanie Klein*, 4 vols. London: Hogarth Press and the Institute of Psychoanalysis.

Winnicott, D.W. (1964) *The Child, the Family and the Outside World*. Harmondsworth: Penguin.

TRANSPERSONAL APPROACHES

Assagioli, R. (1965) *Psychosynthesis: A Manual of Principles and Techniques*. London: Turnstone.

---

while! If you wish to purchase a copy for yourself, the publishers' catalogues often contain order forms and you may order from them directly. A large bookshop may stock the book for which you are seeking and if you are near one, this is the easiest way of

---

Box 2.7 Some publishers of books on counselling and psychotherapy

Constable and Company, 3 The Lanchesters, 162 Fulham Palace Road, London, W6 9ER

Jessica Kingsley Publishers Ltd., 116 Pentonville Road, London, N1 9JB

Open University Press, Celtic Court, 22 Ballmoor, Buckingham, MK18 1XW

Routledge, 11 New Fetter Lane, London, EC4P 4EE

Sage Publications Ltd., 6 Bonhill St., London, EC2A 4PU

---

picking it up. Most of the large chains of bookshops and independent booksellers will be willing to order books for you. If you wish to do this then supply as much information as you can – author, title, publisher and ISBN will all be appreciated. If you are near neither a library nor a bookseller, or just prefer 'armchair shopping', then mail order is an option. Some specialist booksellers offer a mail-order service and they often advertise in the counselling and psychotherapy press. Some of the professional organisations also offer a mail-order bookselling service and these tend to be advertised in their journals or newsletters.

Summary

Every primary training leaves its graduates with gaps in their knowledge. These gaps have priority in any programme of further training. It is important that practitioners address gaps in their training which result in ignorance of or fears or ambivalence about a particular client group or perceived problem.

If a counsellor wishes to change orientation there is no alternative to a substantial training in which the practitioner would get a thorough grounding in the preferred theory and plenty of supervised practice.

Although it is fraught with difficulties, 'self-teaching' is philosophically consistent with the tradition and development of psychotherapy and counselling. An approach to self-teaching could include relevant reading, reflection upon current practice in the light of newly acquired ideas, experience as the client of a practitioner of the 'new' approach and (after discussion with a supervisor) finally the incorporation of the new learning into practice.

The counselling profession lags behind other professional groups in the attention paid to cross-cultural issues. For many counsellors, training in the nature and importance of these issues has been at best sparse – we all have an obligation to address this gap.

Increasingly, and with respect to their practice, counsellors need an awareness of the importance of the law.

Many gaps in training are specific to the individual; to address them is an individual task. Gaps in current knowledge and practice may be identified by systematically posing and answering a number of questions.

There are a number of opportunities to study counselling and therapy at the level of a higher degree. These include both taught courses and research, full and part time. Anyone considering a further qualification should look very carefully at the content and practice requirement of any course to see how it compares with their original qualification. The content of a course and the student's desire to learn from the opportunities it offers are more important than its title.

Training is available in many types of therapeutic endeavour not usually covered in conventional training courses.

Short courses and workshops provide an excellent way of satisfying the 'ongoing training' element of professional development.

Reading is a way in which knowledge may be extended. Classic texts provide a background to counselling in general and to different approaches in particular. Many counselling texts exist, but finding out about them and accessing them is not always easy. Books may be borrowed from libraries, purchased from bookshops, via mail order or direct from the publisher.

3

Professional Recognition: Accreditation and Re-Accreditation

with Alan Frankland

The purpose and nature of professional recognition

Throughout the 1980s and into the 1990s much thought, discussion and debate have taken place with respect to the registration of the practitioners of counselling and psychotherapy. At an organisational level, among the professional associations (and perhaps increasingly, if grudgingly, the profession as a whole) there is widespread agreement on the need for established registers of practitioners. Although this agreement is widespread, it is not universal. Richard Mowbray (1995) has written of the case against registration and challenges many of the widely held beliefs about the reasons for and the advantages of registration.

The intention of registration seems to be to provide an assurance to the public, the profession and the government that registered therapists have undertaken training at a designated level and length, that they are competent practitioners who meet certain standards for supervision and professional development and from whom ethical practice may be expected. There is also a hope to establish modes of professional operation and control before these are imposed by government on less advantageous terms. Mowbray (1995: 10–19) refutes these arguments and states (ibid.: 16) that the government 'does not seem to be very interested' in a statutory register of counsellors or other kinds of psychotherapist. Mowbray's view is that registration is a form of restricted practice which is damaging to the 'human potential movement'.

A further concern is the effect of 'Europeanisation' on the practice of counselling and psychotherapy. Van Deurzen-Smith (1991: 133) in a keynote speech to the BAC conference, offered the view that 'broad European regulations will have a steady sweeping effect on all professions as measures are taken to build equality and equivalence of training and education'. She also discussed the EC general directives applicable to the regulation of professional practice and her view is that some form of registration and/or the recognition of competence in the form of National Vocational Qualifications (NVQs) is inevitable. Her advice was that the professional organisations (specifically the BAC and the UKCP) take a proactive stance on these issues. Because of these pressures, the expectation of the professional organisations is that, sooner or later, the government will wish to establish a national register of practitioners of counselling and psychotherapy. Each organisation wants to influence this procedure on behalf of its members and this contributes to the establishment of registers of 'approved' practitioners. In a chapter entitled 'The European Bogeyman', Mowbray (1995: 20–27) argues that the establishment of the European internal market *does not* call for the registration of professionals.

There is a belief (even a hope) in some quarters that eventually registration will be mandatory. Digby Tantam, current chair of the UKCP, is an advocate of the mandatory registration of psychotherapists. This puts increasing pressure on practitioners to acquire some stamp of approval from at least one of the professional organisations.

Underpinning the idea of a national register of therapists are the various schemes by which the professional organisations offer their members recognition of professional status. The United Kingdom Council for Psychotherapy publishes a register of psychotherapists drawn from the ranks of its constituent organisations. The British Psychological Society now offers suitably qualified members the opportunity to become 'chartered' as

'Counselling Psychologist' and is exploring ways of registering/
recognising psychologists with expertise in other kinds of
psychotherapeutic practice. The BAC has its accreditation
scheme and its register. The Confederation of Scottish Counselling
Agencies (COSCA) is developing an accreditation scheme and the
Association of Christian Counsellors has an accreditation scheme
in place.

Accreditation

> Accreditation in counselling is a benchmark and a burden: a bench-
> mark as it offers public recognition to good practice and protects the
> client from the charlatan; a burden because it absorbs skill, time and
> effort in an attempt to monitor qualities that many feel to be elusive
> and unquantifiable. (Martin et al., 1992: 86)

One of the best-established schemes for the recognition of professional competence as a therapist is the accreditation procedure
of the BAC. This dates from 1983 though (as part of a planned
review procedure) it was suspended for a short while in 1986.
BAC accreditation lasts for five years, after which re-accreditation
is necessary for those who wish to maintain this status.

Even though the demands of BAC members led to the establishment of the accreditation scheme, it has been a source of high
feeling and disagreement since its inception. The correspondence
pages of the BAC journal *Counselling* and its features pages often
address the scheme. The debate has been heated at times and has
included fulsome support, the expression of intense disappointment, queries about relevance and all manner of views betwixt
and between. For instance, Russell and Dexter (1993: 266–269)
use the quotation above and, by examining it point by point, cast
doubt upon accreditation as valuable to the client. Their
preference is for a competency-based measure and they write
of the relevance of NVQs to the assessment of counsellors. Their
paper provoked a response from Foskett (1994: 138) who in turn
casts doubt upon the appropriateness of NVQs to the complex
process of counselling and who argues for the inclusion of clients
in the accreditation process. The issue of accreditation provokes
more intensely personal responses too. Jane Gibbon (1990: 39)
wrote of her own experience of applying for accreditation and
being refused because she did not 'meet the criteria with regard to
training and supervision'. She is critical of what might be a rigid

interpretation of the requirement for theoretical study and points out that, if she had dozed through hours of lectures, she might have met the criterion. Gibbon was asking for a 'case by case' consideration of applications for accreditation rather than the encounter with a rigid bureaucracy which was her experience. From the perspective of the BAC assessors, accreditation is as the result of a process of peer review and it *is* conducted on a 'case by case' basis.

Lambers (1992: 81–82) in a special edition of *Counselling* dealing with accreditation issues, gives an account of the history and process of counsellor accreditation and indicates some of the criticisms made of the scheme. She emphasises the importance of the original aim of the accreditation scheme which she says was the raising and maintaining of standards of training and practice and safeguarding the interests of clients.

Perhaps unfortunately, the accreditation scheme has become linked with notions of quality and competence, and accreditation is increasingly seen as signifying approval. Certainly, it is not uncommon to see advertisements for posts as counselling practitioners which ask that applicants be accredited or eligible for accreditation *as if accreditation is a qualification or guarantee of good practice*. In part this is justified, for the accreditation procedure has always had an element of qualitative assessment and is a kind of qualification. It would be naive, however, to regard qualifications of any kind as a guarantee of good practice. That can only be maintained by other means, for example continuing professional development, ethical practice, supervision, complaints procedures etc.

Since there are many practitioners of counselling who regard themselves as competent, safe and effective therapists but who (for one reason or another) are not accredited, this in itself leads to some resentment. It is not uncommon to hear that accreditation may measure quantity (of training, practice and supervision) but that it falls a long way short of a measure of quality. While it is true that time spent in course attendance doesn't necessarily correspond to learning and that the number of hours of contact with clients and in supervision does not of itself guarantee a high standard of practice, it may be that such global criticisms of the accreditation scheme are at least a little unfair. Through the case studies and the supervisor's report, BAC assessors *do* have some measure of quality.

Box 3.1   BAC accreditation criteria 1994*

Members of the BAC in good standing and who meet the following criteria are eligible for accreditation.

These criteria apply only to counsellors working with individuals or couples. They do not apply to group counselling.

There are **three** routes to Accreditation. The successful candidate will be one who prior to application:

1. (i)   Has completed a BAC recognised Counsellor Training Course *and* has had at least 450 hours of counselling practice supervised in accordance with paragraph 2 below, over a minimum period of three years.

OR

Has undertaken a total of 450 hours of counselling training comprising two elements:

   (a) 200 hours of skills development
   (b) 250 hours of theory

and has had at least 450 hours of counselling practice supervised in accordance with paragraph 2 below, over a minimum period of three years.

OR

   (ii)   Is claiming little formal (course based) counselling training but can provide evidence of seven years' experience in counselling as understood by BAC with a minimum of 150 practice hours per year under formal supervision, *and* has had at least 450 hours of subsequent counselling practice (supervised in accordance with paragraph 2 below), over three years. (NB: this is a restatement of the 'Ten Year Clause'.)

OR

   (iii) Can provide evidence of a combination of:

   (a) some formal counselling training *and*
   (b) several years of practice (of 150 hours minimum per year under formal supervision). This *includes* a requirement for at least 450 hours of counselling practice supervised in accordance with paragraph 2 below, over three years.

   75 hours of *completed* counsellor training = 1 unit
   1 year of supervised practice = 1 unit

   Together the total must add up to 10 units

Applicants claiming two or more training units must show a balance of theory and skills approximately in line with that stated in 1.i.

In addition to the above the applicant is required to meet the following criteria

2. Has an agreed formal arrangement for counselling supervision, as understood by BAC, of a minimum of one and a half hours monthly on the applicant's work, and a commitment to continue this for the period of accreditation.

3. Gives evidence of serious commitment to ongoing professional and personal development such as regular participation in further training courses, study, personal therapy, etc.

4. Is a current member of BAC, and undertakes to remain so for the accreditation period.

5. Has a philosophy of counselling which integrates training, experience, further development and practice. Evidence of at least one core theoretical model should be demonstrated.

6. Demonstrates practice which adheres to the BAC Code of Ethics & Practice for Counsellors and undertakes to continue working within this Code.

Applicants are asked to give evidence of the above in the form of a written application including two case studies. Assessors will be looking for congruence between all parts of the application as well as checking that the above criteria have been and are being met.

* These criteria are reproduced with the permission of the BAC who ask that any readers interested in accreditation refer regularly to that organisation to hear if alterations or additions have been made.

It is true that there are many members of the BAC who *are* excellent practitioners but for whom the accreditation scheme has not been appropriate. In an effort to address this, in 1995 the BAC introduced a third route to accreditation which is more appropriate to counsellors who have some formal training in counselling but who have not attended a training course of the standard and duration of a diploma or master's degree, yet do not have the lengthy experience of counselling practice which might make them eligible for the second route (see Box 3.1).

Preparing for accreditation

> Accreditation is a pain in the rump! (Student counsellor, north-west England as she prepared her application for accreditation)

It may be clear from Box 3.1 that to become accredited is a relatively complex process. This was certainly the view of the counsellor quoted above and I think it is quite common for the experience of preparing for accreditation to be tedious. It is also nerve-racking for at least some counsellors for, in a sense, it involves exposing the whole self to assessment. Accreditation is not only about knowledge, competence and ethics but also about the very intimate areas of philosophy and personal growth. To hold yourself up for examination in all these areas simultaneously takes courage: the experience can be felt as saying to one's peers 'This is me. Am I good enough?' Even though the unsuccessful applicant for accreditation is sent fairly detailed feedback (the accreditation procedure currently involves no face-to-face assessment), to be refused can feel quite humiliating. One counsellor, while somewhat resentfully ploughing her way through her second case study, remarked that if after all this work her application was unsuccessful 'that would be it'. She was successful but it was clear to me that she wondered whether the effort was worthwhile. It is equally true that an increasing number of applicants for accreditation find the process of self-review stimulating and affirming. Although applying for accreditation is a bit daunting, reflecting on development and practice is often experienced as beneficial.

The way in which the accreditation procedure is experienced seems to reflect the attitude the practitioner has to it. Accreditation can be viewed as a suitable challenge, a step in professional development and a learning opportunity in its own right. This can be exciting and stimulating. On the other hand, if the practitioner starts out either feeling it to be unnecessary (perhaps because it is 'obvious' that they merit accreditation) or in fear, then they are likely to experience the process as unpleasant and to lose out on the developmental opportunity it presents.

Each application requires from the applicant a lengthy declaration of their training, philosophy of counselling and personal and professional development and candidates for accreditation are charged a fee. In addition, applicants are required to produce two case studies (one illustrating the use of supervision, the other demonstrating the integration of theory, practice and the espoused philosophy of counselling). Each application must be supported by the counsellor's supervisor and by a referee. Intending applicants for accreditation are (upon request) sent comprehensive guidelines by the BAC. Additionally advice upon preparing an application for accreditation is available from 'consultants' who often are (or have been) BAC convenors. These consultants normally charge for their time and expertise. Occasionally workshops dealing with application for accreditation are offered. At these participants may be offered advice as to the most appropriate route, how to address any shortfall that might lead to their application being unsuccessful, how to write a case study, etc. These workshops are advertised in the counselling press and locally and are a regular feature of the BAC annual training conference. Anyone seriously considering making an application would be well advised to take advice before and during the process, not least because to apply for accreditation involves expenditure; insufficient preparation may lead not only to disappointment but to the loss of hard (and perhaps hard-earned) cash! Frankland (1995: 55–60) points out that, in the past, many unsuccessful applicants for accreditation were not actually eligible. Taking advice and/or undertaking careful research as to the criteria for accreditation *before* spending time and money may save a lot of work and some distress. Frankland's paper is most useful in this respect. The guidelines in Box 3.2 are intended as a useful starting place for anyone considering accreditation but they are no substitute for good advice. Each counsellor is a unique individual and so each application for accreditation is equally unique. Presenting a case for accreditation is not just about mechanically plodding through the 'requirements' – it is about each counsellor presenting themselves as an integrated, responsible and competent practitioner with a coherent philosophy. No amount of general advice can provide the guarantee that any particular individual will do this in the best way for them.

The BAC accreditation scheme is currently undergoing its decennial review. The review is broad and though it is not essentially intended to revise current standards, the range, procedures, relationships with other systems and so on may all undergo development in light of the reviewers' findings. It is possible that the experience-only route will be brought to an end and that additional requirements for personal therapy/counselling

Box 3.2   Guidelines for preparing a submission for accreditation

The basis for these guidelines is the paper by Alan Frankland published in *Counselling*, February, 1995.

1. *Induction*

   Induction is the element of the accreditation system from which assessors are able to infer that an applicant has been adequately prepared for a career in counselling. Broadly speaking, it concerns the applicant's training. This is the element described in section 1 of the accreditation criteria (see Box 3.1). The first task of an applicant for accreditation is to decide which of the three routes is most appropriate for them.

   For applicants who have completed a Recognised Counsellor Training Course, this is a relatively simple matter as the BAC accepts that those who have successfully completed a recognised course meet the requirements for training of the scheme. For applicants for whom this is not the case, the situation is more complex. If an applicant can demonstrate that their training included a substantial course designed to equip them for professional practice in counselling and that their *total* training hours are at least 200 hours of skills development and 250 hours of theory the situation is similar (though the case must be proved).

   Applicants for this route are advised that a 'substantial course' is unlikely to comprise less than 150 contact hours. Assessors may also need to be able to see that the core course (and any additional training) demonstrates a coherent philosophy. Frankland (1995: 57) further advises that short courses (that is those of less than 40 hours) are not normally seen as induction elements but as part of professional and personal development.

   The second route is appropriate to counsellors with many years' experience but little formal training. This route is sometimes called the 'Ten Year Clause'. This route though demands not only that the applicant has been practising counselling for at least ten years' but also specifies a minimum annual amount of supervised practice. This route corresponds to seven years' induction plus three years' counselling experience while in formal supervision as specified in the accreditation criteria.

   The newest route is for applicants who wish to present their induction as a combination of formal training and experience. Here the induction element is calculated in units derived from courses or from years of practice. Applicants must be able to show a total of seven units. A unit comprises either 75 hours of class contact on a completed course or one year of supervised counselling practice of at least 150 hours.

A successful applicant will have satisfied the assessors that they meet one of these criteria in full.

2. *Professional practice experience*

Applicants for accreditation must currently be in practice and have been so for at least six months prior to application with a workload corresponding to 150 hours' client contact a year. It is a condition of accreditation that applicants continue to practise at this level throughout the period of accreditation.

Under whichever induction route an application is made, there is a requirement that the applicants demonstrate that they have completed a substantial amount of counselling practice. For each route this constitutes not less than 450 hours' supervised client contact. The minimum requirement for supervision is one and a half hours a month. This figure applies to *individual* supervision because the prime requirement is for a sound relationship providing adequate presentation time for therapists to explore their relationships with clients. The BAC does accept group supervision as at least contributing to the requirement for supervision but the total that an individual may claim is the amount of time for which the group meets *divided by* the number of people in the group. Thus a counsellor who meets for two hours a month with five colleagues in a facilitated group for the purposes of supervision may claim only 20 minutes (120 minutes divided by 6) as contributing towards the requirement for supervision. The situation for peer groups is similar 'if they are properly contracted, and have the same qualities of maturity and independence' expected of other supervision arrangements. It is probably unwise to rely upon peer group supervision alone to satisfy this requirement.

3. *Probity*

Accreditation is concerned not only with training and amount of practice but also with ethical and professional behaviour. Part of the accreditation process requires that applicants demonstrate their probity in a number of ways. They must show familiarity with and understanding of appropriate codes and demonstrate practice which is in accord with these codes. There is a requirement that probity is attested to by third parties.

Applicants for accreditation must agree to be members of the BAC (and therefore to accept and abide by its codes) and to demonstrate practice which is consonant with the ethical obligations of membership. Any applicant for accreditation who is the subject of an official complaint to the BAC will have their application held over until the complaint is resolved.

Professional probity is in part assured by signed undertakings, in part by the supervisor's report (which includes comment on the applicant's understanding of the codes) and in part by the provision of an appropriate reference. Frankland points out that the diary and case studies that an applicant is required to submit also indicate the nature of practice, 'so the system here does not rely completely on the views/evidence of others, but asks assessors themselves to come to opinions on material supplied by the applicant'. Frankland also states that supervision and continuing professional development are ethical obligations – assessors may consider these elements when deciding upon an applicant's probity.

4. *Practice assessment*
Successful applicants for accreditation will have demonstrated greater effectiveness as counselling practitioners than that expected of novices. In this context, a 'novice' may be assumed to be someone who has successfully completed a counselling training course but has limited client contact. It is important that applicants understand that the assessment of practice does not depend so much upon the *quantity* of practice prior to applying as on a demonstration of effectiveness.

To reach their assessment of an applicant's effectiveness, assessors consider the contribution of initial training *and* 'additional indicators of effectiveness'. The principal evidence used to appraise this aspect of an applicant's ability are the supervisor's report (in which the supervisor is asked to comment upon the standard of the applicant's work with clients) and the one (for graduates of a recognised course) or two case studies which the applicant is required to produce.

Any prospective applicant for accreditation is thus well advised to consult their supervisor at an early stage. An application for which the supervisor's support is less than whole-hearted is unlikely to succeed. In addition, applicants should give some consideration to the writing of case studies. Many counsellors will have written case studies as part of their professional training but even so this can be a daunting task. Parker (1995: 19) has written a paper specifically about how to write a case study and uses the requirements of the BAC accreditation procedure as her model.

5. *Theoretical understanding/clarity*
Assessors expect successful applicants for accreditation to demonstrate a sensible, coherent approach to their counselling. No one theoretical approach is preferred over any other but assessors will look for 'conceptual congruence' and adherence to a core theoretical model. What seems to be important is a degree of consistency between the applicant's training and/or subsequent professional development, the philosophy of the applicant and the way these are carried out in practice with clients. An applicant whose training was

(for example) basically person centred but who declares themselves as holding a psychodynamic view of human nature and whose practice is 'eclectic' may have a much harder job convincing the assessors with respect to this element than someone whose training, philosophy and practice are consistent.

The chief elements on the basis of which theoretical understanding are assessed are the statement of personal philosophy and the case studies. Applicants should ensure that what they say they believe matches what they do. Their knowledge should be adequate to underpin the espoused philosophy and mode of practice.

6. *Continuing professional development*
This is the requirement to demonstrate ongoing efforts to maintain professionalism and effectiveness. Applicants for accreditation are expected to provide evidence of 'output' which might include work for a professional organisation or the dissemination of knowledge as well as 'input' which might include further training or personal therapy. Other chapters in this book should prove useful guides to how this requirement might be satisfied.

7. *Supervision*
Applicants for accreditation are required to have an arrangement for supervision that conforms to the criteria outlined above. In the near future, the BAC may approve a view of 'adequate supervision' which includes a ratio element. This will require trainees to be more intensively supervised than newly qualified practitioners (that is, those in the first three years of practice) who will in turn be required to be more intensively supervised than experienced practitioners. The minimum requirement for one and a half hours' supervision a month is likely to remain.

The BAC has clear reservations about the use of line managers as supervisors (see B.3.3. in the *Code of Ethics and Practice*, 1993). Any applicant whose supervision normally comes from a line manager must have a formalised arrangement with an independent consultant who is suitably qualified and experienced. The counsellor should be able to meet with this consultant at their own discretion.

The requirement for supervision is not met simply by attendance. Through one of the case studies, applicants are required to show how they make use of supervision. Frankland states that assessors are looking for evidence of 'creative and reflective practice' and a real understanding of what supervision is for, and how to put it to use for the benefit of clients.

8. *Other features of the accreditation system*
Besides a consideration of each of the above elements, the assessors of an application for accreditation are looking for coherence of all its parts. There should be agreement between what the applicant says

they do and how they describe a particular piece of work, between training and continuing professional development and philosophy. Assessors are alert for discrepancies in attitudes and values.

> What we are saying is that a mature professional practitioner will be able to reflect on their training and make sense (initially for themselves, but in their application, for others) of the position they have come to and how they arrived there, and will then be able to show that position in action through a case study. They will be able to produce an application that is consistent and congruent, noticing and explaining apparent discrepancies where they arise so that assessors are left with a coherent picture of their philosophy and practice. (Frankland, 1995: 59)

and an expectation that counsellor training should include contextual studies and training in anti-discriminatory practice will be phased in. It is also possible that there will be a development of a 'live' element in the assessment of at least some candidates.

What happens to an application?

Detailed consideration of an application for accreditation is delegated to one of several assessment panels, each of which comprises three assessors and a convenor all of whom are accredited counsellors. Applications are read and assessed in four batches a year and the members of the assessment panel make their decisions independently. An application must be approved by at least three of the assessors on the panel. If two of the assessors find that an applicant has not met the requirements for accreditation and the convenor can assure the Individual Accreditation Group that their assessments coincide and are accurate, then it is most likely that the applicant will not be accredited. The convenor has the additional task of presenting the conclusions of the panel to the Individual Accreditation Group meetings where decisions are made.

Frankland (1995: 60) writes of three possible outcomes. He says that an application may be successful (in which case the counsellor is accredited for five years), deferred or refused. When an application is deferred, it is for clarification or to allow the applicant to make good any minor shortfalls. An application may be refused because the applicant is not practising counselling as understood by the BAC, or because their training, experience or supervision is insufficient, or because they have failed to provide evidence to satisfy assessors on the 'more qualitative elements' such as the case studies and the congruence of philosophy, practice and development. Unsuccessful applicants are sent a 'fairly detailed letter identifying all the grounds on which their application has been refused'. There is a right of appeal on matters both of fact and interpretation. Well over half the applications for accreditation are successful – adequate preparation increases the likelihood that an application will be in this group.

The schemes of the UKCP and the BPS

Among others, two more recognition schemes are relevant to the practice of therapy: the registration procedure of the United Kingdom Council for Psychotherapy and chartering as a counselling psychologist with the British Psychological Society.

The UKCP comprises a number of constituent organisations arrayed in allied sections. These include professional organisations and training institutions. It is only as a registered practitioner of one of these constituent organisations that a therapist becomes eligible to register with the UKCP. The UKCP issues guidelines for training, and constituent organisations which adhere to these guidelines may put forward their qualified members for inclusion on the UKCP register of psychotherapists. Broadly speaking, it is the intention of the UKCP to work towards the position where individuals on the register may be assumed to be trained to a level which corresponds to master's degree and to have substantial practical experience in the model espoused by the constituent organisation to which they belong. Anyone wishing to take this route to professional recognition may expect to undertake a substantial training course (lasting perhaps four or more years) administered or co-ordinated by one of the many organisations belonging to the UKCP. UKCP recognition, like BAC accreditation, lasts for five years and there is an annual registration fee (in 1996) of £45.

The BPS established a division of counselling psychology in 1994. Members of this division who hold a diploma in counselling psychology, or who obtain a statement of equivalence in respect of another training in counselling which is deemed to include training and experience in counselling psychology broadly equivalent to the BPS diploma, are eligible for chartered status but must then make an annual application for a practising certificate. This route to professional recognition is only appropriate to those who hold (or are eligible for) the British Psychological Society's Graduate Basis for Registration, that is those who are graduate psychologists or equivalent.

Summary

There is widespread agreement on the need for established registers of practitioners of counselling and psychotherapy. The purpose of these registers and of accreditation (BAC), registration (UKCP) and chartering (BPS) is to provide an assurance that practitioners with this status are trained and competent and meet established standards for supervision, professional development and ethical practice.

Becoming accredited by the BAC is a relatively complex process. It is not only about demonstrating knowledge, competence and ethics but also about the very intimate areas of philosophy and personal growth.

An applicant for accreditation must make a declaration of their training, philosophy of counselling and professional and personal development. They also submit two case studies and references from their supervisor and a referee.

The BAC produces guidelines for candidates for accreditation and runs workshops dealing with application for accreditation.

An application for accreditation is considered by an assessment panel, all of whom are accredited counsellors. There are three possible outcomes. An application may be successful, deferred or refused. Reasons for deferring or refusing an application are supplied.

The UKCP and the BPS also offer recognition schemes relevant to the practice of therapy. These are open to members of constituent organisations and members of the division of counselling psychology respectively.

4

Personal Therapy

The value of personal therapy

> Purely from my own point of view I would say that perhaps the most
> important aspect of personal therapy has been in 'trusting the process'
> – not as a phrase that is trotted out but as a deeply important experi-
> encing of the meaning of it for myself. (Barbara Douglas, Counselling
> Psychologist, North West Centre for Eating Disorders, personal com-
> munication, 1996)

Personal therapy is widely (but not universally) accepted as a
useful if not essential part of the training of a therapist. This belief
dates back to the earliest days of counselling and psychotherapy.
It is part of our Freudian inheritance and stems from the assumption that only (some of) the analysed are fit to be analysts. Jung
(1966: 132) expressed this well, writing:

> The patient's treatment begins with the doctor, so to speak. Only if the
> doctor knows how to cope with himself (herself) and his own
> problems will he be able to teach the patient to do the same. Only
> then.

From these psychodynamic origins has arisen the belief that, as
a result of the experience in the client role, the therapist may
achieve a higher level of functioning and thus be a more effective
therapist for others. It is only by addressing their own conditions
of worth or repressed and suppressed early experiences or irrational beliefs that therapists become fit persons to accompany
others on the sometimes fearful and painful journey of personal
growth. Although there is little research evidence to support this
view (Aveline, 1990: 334) it remains an article of faith sometimes
so strongly held that its adherents declare it with passion. Ashley,
writing about the practice of psychotherapy states that 'A practitioner who works with an unexamined psyche is as useless as a

pathologist who works with a dirty microscope' (1995: 106). Ashley believes that therapy ('a process which is very costly in time, energy and money') is the *only* way 'of reaching and altering the structure of our innermost selves'. This is not a view universally held even by practitioners of psychodynamic therapies. Goldberg (1992: 42–45) in a survey of the careers of fifty-two psychotherapists found that although some of them greatly valued personal therapy, others were disappointed or even bitter about their experiences. These practitioners indicated that they found life experiences more valuable. A 'considerable number' of the experienced practitioners contacted by Goldberg valued encounters with colleagues, patients, supervisors and 'non-clinical experiences' more than personal therapy. For some of them, spiritual development meant more than earlier experiences of personal therapy. As one therapist said: 'I don't have too much faith in most therapists helping me. Instead, I have opened myself up to a wide range of Eastern philosophies and Western spiritual messages' (quoted in Goldberg, 1992: 44).

My personal experience is that attention to my own personal growth through one-to-one therapy, group therapy and 'co-counselling' has been of great value to me in my work with clients but I would hesitate to say that therapy is the only route to self-understanding and personal transformation. This would seem to deny centuries of knowledge derived from spiritual and religious experience.

Though there may be other paths leading to an integrated state, it might be incumbent on therapists and would-be therapists to make personal use of the practice and philosophy they espouse. This may be especially true because there is some evidence (for example that cited in Guy, 1987: 58–60) to suggest that many trainee therapists have had or do have emotional difficulties. It is also true that the process of training is itself stressful, as Gopelrud (1980: 283–290) discovered. Counselling students often find that they are re-examining their thoughts, feelings, ideals and relationships. Personal therapy can be enormously beneficial in resolving pre-existing difficulties and those thrown up in the process of becoming a therapist. I do wonder, though, if the requirement that therapists in training enter personal therapy is counterproductive. It may conflict with the value attached to consent and perhaps this leads to some of the unhappiness with their personal therapy which some therapists describe.

Gilbert et al. (1989: 7), while stating that they know of no good evidence to show that personal therapy does increase effectiveness, report their experience that many therapists who enter therapy through choice (rather than because it is a requirement of training or accreditation) *do* comment upon their different insight. They say that 'The ability to deal more effectively and honestly with one's own affect is probably central to the development of caring. Coming to know oneself is not always a joyful experience.' Guy (1987) in *The Personal Life of the Psychotherapist*, makes repeated reference (for example p. 161, p. 167, p.264) to the usefulness of personal therapy to the therapist as a means of addressing thoughts and feelings which may hinder effective practice. He also advocates personal therapy as a way of alleviating the stress which may lead to 'burnout'. However, healing and growth are not the only advantages of the personal therapy of the practitioner to client work.

Besides the personal healing and personal growth which may occur in the therapist's own therapy, there is additional valuable learning in the experience of being a client *per se*. We may use the remembrance of our experience to understand something of the thoughts, feelings, doubts and fears of the person sitting opposite us in the client's chair. Guy (1987: 58) records that one of the commonest reasons given for requiring trainee therapists to have personal therapy is that it increases the student's awareness of the therapeutic process. Anthony Storr is an advocate of this view

> I think it is valuable for psychotherapists to be exposed to psychotherapy in order to make it easier for them imaginatively to enter into what their patients are experiencing. (1979: 181)

As well as the insight into the experience of the client which is available through personal therapy, there is learning about the role of therapist. Whether the therapist temporarily occupying the client role is a novice or experienced, they have the opportunity to observe another practitioner in action. This can be most informative. For me as an experienced therapist, the experience of being in therapy with a therapist of a different orientation was both personally and professionally rewarding. Seeing (and feeling) how my therapist worked helped me to look at my own client work from a new perspective. Some of my experiences as a client confirmed my beliefs and affirmed my practices; some of them caused me to question and alter how I interacted with my clients. Dryden and Feltham (1994b: 85–86), writing of the value of using personal therapy as a place to reflect on client work, state that 'Perhaps the main purpose for personal therapy, is to cross-refer actual work with clients with reflections on one's shortcomings, subtle inner resistance and counter transference reactions generally.' Although they are writing about the role of personal therapy in counsellor training and I consider the value of personal therapy to be much wider, what they say is equally true for the experienced practitioner.

Just as personal therapy may be an important part of learning to be a therapist, so it may be an important part of continuing professional development. Again, this belief is traceable to the analytic tradition. For instance:

> Every analyst should periodically – at intervals of five years or so – submit himself to analysis once more, without feeling ashamed of taking this step. This would mean, then, that not only the therapeutic analysis of patients but his own analysis would change from a terminable into an interminable task. (Freud, 1937/1964: 249)

I do not agree with the time interval indicated by Freud, but I certainly agree that therapists have a continual (but not necessarily continuous) obligation to tend to their own needs, and an appropriate way of doing this is through personal therapy.

The various professional bodies make clear their appreciation of the value of personal therapy as part of continuing professional development. This is in part a recognition of the learning potential in the client role but it is also about maintaining emotional and mental fitness and countering pressures which may lead to burnout, loss of effectiveness or even abusive behaviour. Wood et al. (1985) in a survey of 167 psychotherapists found that 4.2 per cent acknowledged problems with substance abuse, 0.6 per cent had indulged in 'sexual misconduct' with clients and 32.3 per cent experienced depression and burnout significant enough to interfere with clinical work. Similarly, Norcross and Prochaska (1986) in a survey of female therapists and lay persons, found that approximately 80 per cent of the therapists had experienced at least one episode of 'high distress' in the previous three years. These findings are reflected in other studies, as is the finding that therapists are reluctant to enter therapy. This reluctance is worrying for it suggests that either therapists are complacent about their own abilities, are ashamed of needing therapy (or believe that they will be seen in an ill light if they become clients), have doubts about the efficacy of therapy, or some combination of these. Whatever the reason, the therapists who suffer incapacitating emotional distress and yet do not avail themselves of the services of a therapist are giving a most disconcerting message to both clients and peers. Norcross and Guy (1989: 234) indicate that, in fact, some therapists *do* avail themselves of the services they provide (they quote figures to suggest that over 50 per cent of therapists use some kind of therapeutic service after they are qualified and practising) – it's just that they keep quiet about it! Perhaps it is time we stood up to be counted. If we do not demonstrate our belief in the efficacy of our own profession how can we expect anyone else to?

For me, there is an analogy between the professional obligation of therapists to pay constant attention to their mental, emotional, spiritual (and, yes, even physical) state, to maintain their fitness and continue their growth, and the obligation of an athlete to maintain a peak of physical fitness and mental stamina. Just as athletes expect to train and to treat their bodies with respect, avoiding both over-indulgence and neglect in order to ensure a good and improving performance, so should therapists. We have an obligation to care for ourselves (if we don't, how can we expect our clients to care for themselves?), and to continue our efforts to keep ourselves emotionally and/or cognitively fit. Personal therapy or personal growth is a way of ensuring that fitness and is the equivalent of circuit training for the athlete. This belief is echoed by other therapists. For instance: 'Personal therapy provides an opportunity for self-awareness, self-assessment, rejuvenation, reality-testing, and replenishment' (Guy, 1987: 264).

Rowan states that he has his own therapist, whom he sees twice a week. He writes:

> It is essential to me to have somewhere to go with my distress or my lack of understanding, and be enabled to work through it and come out with some better awareness of what has been going on. (Rowan, 1989: 164)

The recognition that Rowan has of his need for a place to resolve his personal and professional issues is something from which all therapists could learn. Even the most eminent therapists are vulnerable to the pressures and strains of the profession and of life in general. Marcia Karp (1991: 3–10) one of the leading psychodramatists in Britain, has written most movingly of her experience of depression and how that impinged upon her professional work, her family, her friends and her essential self. She also wrote: 'The greatest professional hazard to which I have been prey is to feel unreachable and beyond help' (1989: 100). She warns against this 'irrational yet real condition' and offers a list of danger signals which may indicate it.

The experience of practitioners indicates that personal therapy facilitates the task of the professional therapist. The professional organisations look favourably upon personal therapy and structured personal growth as valid contributions to professional development. Therapy provides a space in which the practitioner can unburden, deal with the strains brought about by practice and those life stresses which impinge upon effective practice. It may also be a place to reflect on client work. Furthermore, besides being about support, learning and restoration, personal therapy is about *growth*. A satisfactory course of therapy will not only restore the distressed practitioner to effective practice but may resource them to be *more effective*. This means that therapy is appropriate when the therapist is aware of less efficient functioning stemming from emotional distress or preoccupation and that it is equally appropriate when the therapist feels in good form. It may be that the practitioner who enters therapy without a pressing and immediate emotional need is better placed to use the interaction for growth. Given all this, how is a practitioner to make a choice from the range of therapies and therapists with which they are confronted?

Choosing a therapist

In choosing a therapist, there are many issues to consider and the choice tends to be an intensely personal one. For many prospective clients (including counsellors) it is the personal characteristics of the therapist that are most important. Warmth, experience and personality might be more important than any other factors. This aside, perhaps prime considerations are cost and the reputation (see Box 4.1) of the therapist. Secondary considerations may include the orientation and mode of practice of the therapist, the availability of a suitable therapist, the practitioner's aims and

---

Box 4.1   Choosing a reputable therapist

In choosing a therapist, the practitioner might like to be certain that the chosen person:

- belongs to a bona fide professional organisation appropriate to the nature of the therapy being offered and which has a published code of ethics;
- is in supervision for their client work;
- is clear about the terms and conditions of the contract for therapy;
- is adequately trained and/or experienced.

---

intentions in entering therapy and the most suitable pattern of attendance for the would-be client.

Cost

For most of us, cost is an issue. One-to-one therapy can be expensive, perhaps costing between £20 and £35 per session, although there are therapists who charge less and others who charge more. Most of us must balance our aims and needs for therapy against our ability to pay. Depending upon the intention with which the practitioner enters therapy, it may not be that more costly equals better. If the practitioner wishes to be a psychoanalyst, then there is no alternative to a course of analysis lasting several years and costing thousands of pounds. If the need is less rigidly defined, perhaps there are relatively cheap ways of meeting it. As a general rule, group therapy tends to be cheaper than one-to-one therapy. This is for the very obvious reason that the cost of the therapist's (or more likely two or more co-therapists') time is defrayed amongst more individuals. The downside of this would appear to be that each person in the client role gets less of the therapist's attention pro rata. This may be less important than it seems for group therapy has much to offer other than the attention of the therapist(s) (see pp. 76–79), and groups tend to meet for longer sessions.

There are other ways in which the impoverished practitioner may have access to cheaper (or even free) therapy. If the need is acute, then counselling may be available through the NHS (an increasing number of general practitioners provide counselling among their range of services or are able to make and pay for referrals elsewhere), a voluntary organisation or an employer. These are unlikely to meet the need of someone whose intent is personal growth and the exploration of a relatively healthy psyche but may be appropriate in times of emotional distress. Some therapists offer sessions at a reduced rate for those experiencing financial hardship, sometimes even allocating a proportion of their work time to 'public service'. Therapists who take this attitude may be willing to work with another therapist whose main aim is continuing development but who is of restricted means. Lastly, it may be possible to enter into a reciprocal arrangement with another therapist or group of therapists in which 'co-counselling' is offered. In the absence of any other arrangement, and providing it is well supervised, such a co-counselling arrangement may be fruitful.

Reputation

How does the practitioner who wishes to enter personal therapy contact a reputable, suitable and effective therapist? There are directories and registers published by the professional organisations (such as the BAC and the UKCP) which contain the names and addresses of practitioners and sometimes additional details such as orientation, fee, specialist interests and training. These are available from the organisations themselves or in bigger public libraries. These publications do not necessarily guarantee the quality or ability of the practitioner. Inclusion indicates only that the practitioners included subscribe to the codes of ethics and professional conduct of the organisation and are members in good standing. For instance, therapists who appear in the BAC directory have paid for their entry and what they say of themselves must be taken on trust. The inclusion of a therapist in, for instance, the register of the UKCP, BPS or BAC *does* imply certain levels of training and experience and that ethical and professional practice may be expected of them. Therapists who are accredited, chartered or registered will usually say so in any directory listing or other form of publicity. Such publicity may be found in counselling and therapy publications, 'alternative' magazines, the windows of whole-food shops, the noticeboards of public libraries, community centres, therapy centres and places where complementary medicine is practised. Indeed, where a therapist chooses to advertise might itself tell the prospective client something about them.

Although therapists do advertise and professional organisations produce lists of practitioners, personal recommendation is still a basis for the choice of therapist made by many clients, not least by people who are themselves in practice. So little can be told of the nature and ability of a therapist from a directory entry that the recommendation of a friend, colleague or supervisor is often preferred. Any practitioners considering entering personal therapy would be well-advised to discuss this with their supervisor. Such a discussion may help the practitioner clarify the aims they have in therapy and therefore bring them closer to identifying a suitable therapist. Issues which may be important to reflect upon include the gender of the likely therapist, the unresolved issues known to the practitioner and/or the supervisor and any special circumstances of the practitioner (is it important that a potential therapist shares these special circumstances?). Once the practitioner can come closer to describing the characteristics of their preferred therapist, it may be that the supervisor is better able to make a recommendation, or at least it may narrow the field.

Regardless of personal recommendation or professional status, there is an important element of subjective choice involved in the selection of a therapist. In the final stages of this selection, there is no substitute for a face-to-face meeting in the therapist's place of practice. Most therapists will agree to an initial meeting with no further obligation to either party, and some insist on it. Attitudes to payment for this session differ widely. Some therapists make no charge for such a meeting, most charge their standard fee and some charge more. A preliminary meeting can be used to check many things. These may include the nature of the issues the practitioner expects to bring to therapy but perhaps most important is the purely subjective judgements: 'Do I trust and feel comfortable enough with this person?' and 'Can I envisage myself doing the personal work I want to do here and with this person?'

Orientation

The issue of the orientation of the chosen therapist is complex and the orientations from which to choose are many. Rowan and Dryden (1988: 5) produce a diagram entitled 'The Therapeutic Space' in which they relate therapies to two dimensions (attention paid to the conscious/unconscious and a spiritual dimension). In this diagram, they include thirty-five different orientations and this excludes most of the creative approaches, newer approaches such as cognitive analytic therapy and some longer established approaches such as multimodal therapy. The would-be client is likely to have a choice of over fifty orientations. There are therapies which are relevant to intellectual, left-brain under-standing, ones which are relevant to right-brain synthesis; there are therapies which deal with spiritual aspects of human beings, those that stress the importance of the unconscious and those that don't. Some therapies are largely experiential, allowing subtle personal meanings to be drawn and placing little weight on 'understanding', while some value rationality highly. How might the choice be made?

Broadly speaking, there are arguments in favour of being in therapy with a practitioner of the same (or similar) orientation and arguments in favour of being in therapy with a practitioner of a different orientation. Being in therapy with a therapist of the same orientation can be affirming and instructive. It is especially important that therapists at the beginning of their careers take this path because learning or consolidating practice of one orientation and yet being on the receiving end of another can be confusing. Dryden and Feltham (1994b: 72), discussing the personal therapy of trainee counsellors, consider that 'the rule of thumb here is that personal therapy experiences should not be too dissimilar to the core model'. For a more experienced therapist or one who is sure of their chosen orientation, there can be advantages in being the client of a therapist of a different orientation, *providing that the value system and the model of the person on which this other orientation is predicated is not so irksome to the client as to interfere with the process of therapy.* These advantages include the perspective the practitioner can bring to their own model and a deeper understanding of the strengths and weaknesses of each.

There may be other reasons for selecting a therapist of a different orientation. Above, I discussed the advantages of choosing a therapist of the 'new' orientation for the practitioner wishing to make a change. This is a sound way of getting to know more about any particular approach. The personal needs of the practitioner may also indicate a suitable orientation. Some approaches may be more appropriate to some intentions than others. For example anyone seeking a therapy which will attempt to address deep-seated issues from the past might be advised to try a psychodynamic therapy or even primal integration. If the issues to be addressed lie more in the area of present-day problems, perhaps one of the cognitive behavioural approaches would be suitable. The range of humanistic and transpersonal approaches to therapy might be more appropriate for issues of purpose and meaning or spirituality, and therapies based on a systemic approach for family issues. Each of these groups of therapies offers insight into different aspects of being a person, so experiencing something of therapies which address the unconscious, thinking, subjective, here-and-now experience, transpersonal issues and the creative or expressive aspects of human nature may contribute to professional development as well as personal development.

Then there is the issue of familiarity and adroitness. Kottler (1986: 122) writes:

> Many therapists are well versed in the techniques of avoiding therapeutic experiences . . . When it comes to changing our own behaviour, we are perfectly skilled at pretence and acting.

I recognise this tendency in myself and in others – but I think it is seldom intentional; rather it arises from a degree of familiarity with technique and process which allows defences to be very effective. There may be advantages in going to a therapist who uses a form of therapy very different from that of the practitioners themselves. For instance, I am quite skilled with words and in this mode of expression my 'resistance and defences' are especially strong. I am not nearly so able with colour, shape and form. When I have taken part in art therapy, I have been surprised at the power, relevance and personal meaning of the images I have produced. I have reached insights quite different from those I have reached in 'talking' therapies, and in a shorter time. It isn't that art therapy is 'better', but it is different – and that difference is sometimes facilitative.

Mode of practice/method of delivery

Therapy is offered one to one, in small groups and large groups. It is offered regularly (usually once a week but also less and more often) and in the form of intensive but occasional blocks (days, weekends, weeks or perhaps longer). It is even possible to combine personal therapy with a holiday in the sun! There are therapists who direct, therapists who teach, therapists who facilitate, therapists who guide (guide is the preferred title of psychosynthesis practitioners and it relates to their work with a spiritual dimension), there are therapists who offer interpretations and those who offer a holistic experience. The form in which therapy is offered may depend upon the orientation of the practitioner (psychodrama, for instance, is most likely to be offered to a group) but for most orientations there are one-to-one forms and group variants. Groups may be offered on a regular basis or as 'intensives' lasting a day, a weekend or longer and these intensives may or may not be residential. Groups that run regularly may be either closed (unavailable to new members once the contract has begun) or open (new members may join at any time). Every form has advantages and disadvantages in comparison to the others.

Individual therapy

Individual therapy offers privacy and confidentiality of a high degree. What is said and done is heard and observed by one other person and relayed (at most) to the therapist's supervisor. In individual therapy, the client can expect the undivided attention of the therapist. Many people value this protected encounter and the minimal exposure it brings – it is the right atmosphere for them to engage in deep, revealing self-exploration. Because of the nature of the contract and the ethical and professional standards of the therapist, levels of acceptance may be expected of individual therapy which are not necessarily available from peers in a therapy group.

This intimacy and privacy may be appropriate to many people and for many issues, but there is a downside. Individual therapy tends to be more costly than group therapy and the price of intimacy is the lack of learning about others and about the self in relation to others.

Group therapy

Small group therapy in which the group meets weekly is the most common form of group therapy. In this context 'small' group is said by Aveline and Dryden (1988: 7) to comprise seven to ten people. I think that their maximum number is on the low side. For instance, in my work as a psychodramatist I would consider a group of fifteen to be quite manageable but most viable groups have between six and twelve members. Such groups are offered by therapists of many orientations. Those described in Aveline and Dryden (1988) include four analytic group therapies, interpersonal, cognitive behavioural and Gestalt group therapy and psychodrama. Corey (1994) includes Adlerian, existential, person centred, transactional analysis, behavioural, rational emotive and reality therapy approaches to group work and (ibid.: 487, 491–492) produces useful charts showing the different group goals and techniques used in each of these approaches. To these may be added expressive and creative group therapies (such as dance-movement therapy, dramatherapy and art therapy) and encounter. All of these and more (including, for instance, neuro-linguistic programming) are offered as intensive workshops.

A session of a small group will cost perhaps half as much as a one-to-one session and last twice as long. In terms of unit cost, one-off intensives are probably even cheaper. A two or two-and-a-half-hour small group session may cost between £10 and £20 but a day experiential group (six to eight hours) will cost between £30 and £50, though many group therapists will take more group members in one-off groups.

Price is not the only advantage offered to the practitioner by group therapy. Mearns (1994: 36) considers that, for the person centred counsellor in training,

> The experience of 200 hours of experiential groups is much preferred to 200 hours of personal therapy because the public perception of the trainee becomes part of the agenda as well as issues which are raised by the trainee herself.

Bloch (1988: 299–308) is cautious in his answer to the question 'Is group therapy effective?' – a question he thinks is not worth asking in that form because 'group therapy' is a general term for a number of not always similar approaches and because it excludes the notion of for whom group therapy might be effective. Orlinsky and Howard (1978: 310–311) report that the great majority of outcome studies addressing the relative efficacy of group therapy versus individual therapy show no significant differences between the two. They further report that some studies have found that group therapy is significantly better than individual therapy and that two studies indicate that a combination is favoured.

Group therapy has a great deal to offer both the beginning and experienced practitioner. I extend Mearns's arguments to group approaches to therapy in general because they all offer the opportunity for participants to learn about themselves, themselves in relation to others, and human communication and interactions in general. Growth in groups depends not just upon interaction between the client and the therapist(s) but on all the other interactions as well.

In a psychodrama group, for instance, the facilitator will work with one person (the protagonist) to develop a scene. Some other members of the group (now auxiliaries) take roles within that scene while the remainder (the audience) watch the unfolding action. The protagonist explores a personal issue and may move towards understanding or resolution, the auxiliaries have the experience of exploring another way of being (which may or may not be familiar) and even the 'passive' audience may be making strong personal connections with the story they are witnessing – indeed, this is more often the case than not. Whatever the style of the group, all these things are possible. Sometimes learning and growth are the result of being the focus of attention, sometimes they are the result of being closely involved with somebody else's work, sometimes they are the outcome of an apparently more passive process.

These opportunities do not represent the limits of the power of group therapy. Jan Costa (personal communication, 1994) an experienced group therapist who, amongst her other clients, works with adults who have been abused as children, speaks of the importance of giving testimony and witnessing to the process of healing. By this she means that it is important that the person in the client role give an account of their traumatic, hurtful or damaging experiences (testimony) and that these are heard by others (witnessing). Of course this happens in individual therapy but in her experience (and in mine) the process is more powerful when there are more witnesses and the witnesses are peers.

Although the 'once a week' model of group therapy pre-dominates, there may be advantages in considering the role of intensive, one-off sessions or therapy offered intermittently (for example once a month). There is little evidence to indicate that weekly therapy is 'better' than any other kind and Kellerman (1992: 21) cites evidence to suggest that the reverse might be true. The advantages of patterns of attendance other than a weekly ongoing group may include cost and convenience. It may be easier to attend an occasional weekend group than one that meets weekly.

The disadvantages of group therapy include the more limited access to the time and attention of the therapist(s) and the higher degree of exposure. Because group members are in some way making a commitment to each other, groups may not be suitable for someone who is in acute need.

Co-counselling

Although co-counselling (in, for instance, the form of re-evaluation counselling – see Evison and Horobin, 1988: 85–109) is an approach to therapy in its own right, and one which the practitioner seeking personal therapy might wish to consider, I am using the term here for any reciprocal arrangement which two or more therapists may make in order to offer each other personal therapy. This could take the form common to co-counselling proper where the time in a session is equally divided between two people who each have a turn in the client role, or it could be structured differently. For instance, three therapists could come to a mutual agreement in which each was the client of one of the others and therapist to the remaining one. This acting as therapist and as client to one's peers is something with which many therapists are familiar from their training.

An advantage of such arrangements is that the cost is minimal (perhaps only that of supervision) but co-counselling involves a level of responsibility on the part of the 'client' which is absent from other forms of therapy.

Alternatives to personal therapy

The objectives of personal therapy include the maintenance of psychological, emotional and spiritual health, increasing under-standing of human nature and personal growth, and there might be other ways of achieving each or all of these. These include journal keeping, stress management, meditation and providing time and space for 'rest and recreation'. Such strategies are considered in Chapter 7 'Resourcing Your Self'.

Summary

From the earliest days of counselling and psychotherapy, personal therapy has been widely accepted as an essential part of the training and development of a therapist. It is consistent for therapists and would-be therapists to make personal use of the practice and philosophy they espouse.

Personal therapy provides valuable learning about the experience of being a client and the opportunity to observe another practitioner in action.

Professional bodies appreciate personal therapy as part of continuing development. This is in part a recognition of its learning potential but it is also about maintaining emotional and mental fitness countering pressures which may lead to burnout, loss of effectiveness or even abusive behaviour.

Choosing a therapist is an intensely personal task. Cost, reputation, orientation and mode of practice are all issues to consider.

Individual therapy, group therapy, and co-counselling all have their advantages and disadvantages.

Alternatives to personal therapy include stress management, meditation and relaxation which are considered in Chapter 7.

5

Supervision

Supervision is an important part of the professional life of any therapist and Stoltenberg and Delworth (1987) regard it as having developmental stages. Page and Wosket (1994: 5–6) regard the trainee counsellor as moving through a series of clearly defined developmental stages which are defined in terms of the counsellor's 'growing competence and awareness'. The stages in Box 5.1 I have adapted from those recognised by Page and Wosket (1994: 7; after Stoltenberg and Delworth).

Professional organisations require members to be in supervision. This is seen as a safeguard for both client and therapist. Hawkins and Shohet (1989: 42) cite Brigid Proctor as describing three principal functions of supervision. These are:

- educative or formative
- supportive or restorative
- managerial or normative

All of these, especially the formative function, may relate to professional development.

Proctor (1994: 313) writes that 'Supervisor and counsellor share responsibility for promoting the personal well-being of the counsellor . . . as well as her professional development and professional accountability' and (ibid.: 311–312) she gives characteristics of good and bad supervisory practice. Her important features of a good session include:

- offering effective challenge in furtherance of the working agreement.

Box 5.1   Developmental stages in counsellor supervision

1. A 'beginner' stage in which the practitioner or trainee is anxious and dependent on the supervisor. There is little awareness of self and self in relation to others and the expressed need is for specific interventions and 'answers'. A primary concern is with 'doing it right'. The supervisor is seen as teacher, monitor and possibly censor. The role of the supervisor is to provide support, offer knowledge of techniques and to be clear about ethical and professional boundaries.

2. A 'probationer' stage in which the practitioner is beginning to integrate theoretical learning and experience from practice. The relationship between therapist and supervisor shares something with that between parent and teenager. Sometimes a high degree of dependence is displayed, sometimes an almost inappropriate degree of autonomy. This is the stage at which practitioners begin to develop their own identity, to take risks and to experiment with the techniques available to them. The supervisor's function is to 'contain' the counsellor and to be watchfully supportive of the struggle for independence and professional individuality.

3. The 'journeyman' stage in which the practitioner is 'good enough'. There is a greater sense of professional identity, an awareness of strengths and limitations and confidence in abilities. All this contributes to the therapeutic use of self. With the professional and personal confidence comes a greater openness to the ideas and practices of counsellors of other orientations. The supervisor is now more a collaborator than an educator or manager. Attention is increasingly paid to process rather than to technique.

4. The 'master therapist' (which Stoltenberg and Delworth say is a stage not achieved by all). At this stage, practitioners are displaying high levels of autonomy, are insightful and personally secure and are accepting of challenges from themselves and others. The supervisor for a therapist at this stage is seen as a peer and the relationship that of equals – the direction of the supervision session is shared.

- communicating awareness of contextual issues which affect either the counselling or the supervision session (for example ongoing issues such as a client's physical disability, or immediate issues such as the mutual anxiety of the assessment process).
- a framework for understanding the unspoken process and agendas, and an ability to use that understanding in order to further the task of the session.

- an ability to share ideas, frameworks and experiences in a way that is helpful to the supervisee.

Each of these pertains to the professional development of the supervisee.

In their book about developing supervision, Feltham and Dryden (1994: 73–88) devote a chapter to the developmental opportunities of supervision. These are to:

1. Focus on and challenge supervisees' grasp of theory and translation of theory into practice.
2. Challenge supervisees on the possible limitations of their approach with particular clients.
3. Be aware of research findings and professional developments and encourage supervisees to acquaint themselves with these when it is helpful to do so.
4. Suggest that supervisees undertake further training, reading and personal development work as necessary.
5. Share your own clinical and developmental experiences with supervisees when it is helpful to do so.

Clearly, supervision has great potential as an agent for the continuing development of any practitioner, so choosing an appropriate supervisor is a matter of importance.

Choosing a supervisor

Except for the fact that there is a professional obligation of counsellors to be in supervision, choosing a supervisor is similar to choosing a personal therapist. The practitioner will pose the same questions (for example the same or different orientation?) and face the same difficulties (how to make contact with a suitable, affordable supervisor). Matters to consider include the orientation, training (in supervision) and experience of the potential supervisor, the cost and frequency of supervision, and the style (that is, individual, group or peer group supervision).

There are now a number of courses offering a training in supervision and the BAC has an accreditation scheme for suitably qualified and experienced supervisors. An increasing number of people offering supervision are graduates of such a course and

a smaller number are 'accredited' supervisors. Most people practising as supervisors are doing so on the basis of their experience
as (in the first instance) practitioners and as supervisees
themselves. Choosing an accredited supervisor, like choosing an
accredited counsellor or recognised psychotherapist, offers a
guarantee that the supervisor has received some form of training
in supervision and has satisfied a group of peers (through the
presentation of case material and a live assessment) of their
supervisory skills. A trained supervisor (but one who is not
accredited) may also be assumed to have satisfied some assessment procedure. In the absence of any other recommendation or
criteria, choosing a supervisor who has undergone some assessment may offer the supervisee a degree of 'safety' but it does
considerably limit the choices. Good or even excellent supervision is available from people who have not undertaken any
formal training or put themselves forward for accreditation. Such
supervisors are usually found as a result of the advice of
colleagues or some other personal contact. Perhaps the recommendation of someone who is trusted by and knows the
supervisee and the supervisor is worth as much as the promise
held out by training or recognition.

Though there are many issues to consider in the selection of a
supervisor (see Hawkins and Shohet, 1989: 16–30) a principal
concern of this chapter is how to maximise the developmental
opportunities of supervision. Many authors (for example Hawkins
and Shohet, 1989; Goldberg, 1992; Skovholt and Ronnestad, 1995)
describe stages in the development of therapists/ supervisees and
some of these schemata are described and discussed by Feltham
and Dryden (1994: 14–17). There is broad agreement that the
developmental needs of supervisees differ with their degree of
experience. This leads to the conclusion that a beginning therapist
will require a different form of supervision (and perhaps a
different supervisor) from a more experienced therapist. The issue
of the supervisor's orientation is a good example. Beginning
therapists who are as yet unsure of the limits and advantages of
their own model may find the views of a supervisor of a different
orientation confusing, while an experienced therapist may very
well find a different viewpoint stimulating. For example, students
on the person centred course with which I have been associated
have sometimes reported their confusion when supervisors have
offered them psychodynamic insights. Sometimes, to their

Box 5.2 Limitations of individual supervision (from Feltham and Dryden, 1994: 46)

- The supervisee receives the input of only one other person, which may sometimes be unhelpfully biased.

- Supervisor and supervisee may share the same views too closely and thus unconsciously develop a collusive relationship.

- The supervisee does not have the opportunity to compare his or her work with other counsellors, particularly those at the same developmental stage.

---

detriment, this confusion has carried over to and affected their assessed work. Once students are surer of themselves (usually as a result of plenty of practice), they tend to find other perspectives helpful. This may be similar for more experienced therapists. As a person centred therapist I have for some years been in supervision with a very experienced supervisor whose orientation is psychodynamic. I haven't always agreed with her understanding of my clients but even thinking about why I disagreed has been helpful and, for the most part, her different perspective has benefited me and my clients.

Individual supervision has many strengths (Feltham and Dryden, 1994: 45) and provides the least time-consuming way of meeting the BAC requirement that accredited counsellors be in supervision for at least one and a half hours per month. A supervisor chosen with the developmental aspects of supervision in mind will offer the supervisee many opportunities for growth and learning. This seems to be a common experience. Norcross and Guy (1989: 227) in their survey of ten therapists, report that the aspect of their training experience which was most commonly recognised by themselves as important was clinical supervision. Similarly, students on the course with which I have been associated almost without fail rate field supervision as a particularly significant and valuable part of their development. I believe that this significance continues throughout the professional life of any therapist.

However, perhaps especially with respect to professional development, individual supervision has its limitations. Some of these are listed in Box 5.2.

In the view of many practitioners and the BAC, individual supervision offers the most effective way of protecting supervisees

and their clients because in a sound supervisory alliance supervisees are able to use the whole supervision session to present
and explore their own clients in a safe and confidential setting. I
don't dispute the value of individual supervision but I agree with
Feltham and Dryden that it has its shortcomings. Other forms of
supervision (for example group supervision), while having
limitations of their own may offer ways of addressing these
shortcomings and so be valuable in the process of professional
development.

Group supervision

> Groups clearly have many advantages over individual supervision in
> the range of possible learning opportunities and different perspectives
> that they can provide. (Hawkins and Shohet, 1989: 107)

For the purposes of this discussion, group supervision occurs
when a group of practitioners meet together in the presence of a
facilitator/supervisor to present and discuss their clients. Such
groups may be constituted of therapists of the same orientation
and approximately the same level of professional development or
they may be heterogeneous. Group supervision offers the supervisee access to a wider variety of expertise, experience and
opinion than does individual supervision. In a group setting, the
supervisee has the opportunity to present case material to a
number of people and to receive input, support and feedback
from a number of perspectives. This can be stimulating and
exciting and certainly offers a lot to think about. The role of the
facilitator varies according to the orientation and purpose of the
group but generally speaking it is a role analogous to that of a
group therapist. Facilitators will not usually present their own case
material but will respond to the material presented and to the
presenter in a manner consistent with the task of supervision and
the orientation they espouse. Because the cost of the facilitator's
time is defrayed among the group members, group supervision
tends to be appreciably cheaper than individual supervision
(although it may not be the most economical way of meeting the
BAC requirement for supervision).

Whereas in individual supervision the supervisees consider only
their own clients, in group supervision there is an opportunity to
hear about the clients and practice of other therapists. Even in this

relatively passive role there are developmental opportunities but there are additional advantages because each member of the group is in effect a co-supervisor for every other member. This more active role requires that the practitioner reflect upon and, where appropriate, respond to the material being presented. So in group supervision, each member of the group benefits not only from presenting and exploring clients of their own but also from the active consideration of presentations of other members of the group.

In 1995, the professional sub-committee of the BAC reviewed the requirements of supervision for members of the BAC and accredited counsellors (indicating that these were not necessarily the same). The interim results of this review were published in *Counselling*, (6 (3): 171–172) and a review of the 'value ' of group supervision was included. In the view of the sub-committee, the existing requirement for supervision 'fails to take account of how, in group supervision, learning takes place from cases presented by all members of the group. It is very clear that numerous members want this to be recognised.'

The sub-committee accepted this view and proposed a formula by which the contribution of group supervision to the BAC requirement could be calculated. This formula was a function of the size of the group, the experience of the supervisee and the time spent in group supervision. This is an acknowledgement of the additional learning opportunities in group supervision and a suggestion that more experienced therapists derive more benefit from it than do therapists in early stages of development (or perhaps that experienced therapists need less individual supervision than trainees and 'probationers'?). This paper (which was intended as a discussion document) also contains the assertion that no supervision group should comprise more than six supervisees, with the implication that any time spent in bigger supervision groups would be discounted, for the purposes of accreditation at least.

Group supervision also offers the possibility of using the group members creatively to explore client/therapist relationships. Feltham and Dryden (1994: 46) consider that one of the benefits of group supervision is that experimentation with role play may be possible. Hawkins and Shohet (1989: 96–97) also write of the opportunity to use action techniques as an advantage of group supervision. Elsewhere (Wilkins, 1995) I have described a creative therapies model for group supervision and, with the above authors, I see that the opportunity to re-enact particular aspects of the client/therapist relationship and to use creative techniques to explore the forces acting on that relationship and/or strategies for working with a particular client as one very fruitful form of group supervision.

Group supervision is not without its drawbacks. Feltham and Dryden (1994: 47) and Hawkins and Shohet (1989: 98) describe some of the disadvantages. These include the fact that there is obviously less time for each member of the group to present material than there would be in individual supervision and that the dynamics of the group may become a complicating factor. The extent to which this interferes with the process of supervision may very well depend upon the skills of the facilitator.

Hawkins and Shohet also consider that the dynamics of the client/therapist relationship are less likely to emerge in group supervision. In my experience working psychodramatically as a group supervisor, the process between the supervisee and the client is often reflected in the process between me and the supervisee. Indeed it may be more obvious and more tractable than in individual supervision and I regard this as one of the advantages of group supervision.

Group supervision then may offer a useful adjunct to individual supervision, particularly as a way to meet some developmental needs. A therapist contemplating joining a supervision group may wish to consider a number of matters before making that commitment. By its very nature, group supervision can be more 'exposing' than individual supervision. It is likely to lack the intimacy and (for some) the sense of safety that one-to-one supervision can offer. This is compensated for by the richness of experience and opinion among the group members, but just as for some clients individual therapy is the preferred form so group supervision is not appropriate for all therapists. If the benefits seem to outweigh the disadvantages then the potential group supervisee may like to pose the questions in Box 5.3.

Peer supervision

Peer supervision is only suitable for more experienced counsellors. (Professional sub-committee of the BAC, *Counselling*, 6 (3): 172)

Box 5.3   Questions to ask about group supervision

- At my stage of development, would I benefit most from a group comprising therapists of different orientations or from a group of my peers?

- Do I want to join a structured group in which the time is equally shared between its members or do I want something less structured?

- How long am I prepared to wait for my turn to present? This may be a function of group size and/or the way the group is structured. Hawkins and Shohet (1989: 97) consider that a supervision group should comprise at least three supervisees but no more than seven (otherwise they have to fight for time and attention). I think that this depends upon the purpose of the group and for how long and how regularly it meets.

- What do I want from the group facilitator and what evidence is there that I'm likely to get what I want? Issues to consider include orientation, expertise, experience and training.

- Do I want to join a group that will take a creative approach to the exploration of the client/therapist relationship?

- How are issues of group dynamics likely to be dealt with in the group?

Just as there is a personal or intuitive element in the selection of a therapist or individual supervisor so there is in the selection of a group supervisor and a supervision group. It is important that the supervisee feels trusting enough of the facilitator and the group to be able to present client work and to offer feedback and support to others.

A third form of supervision is that between peers. This may be either on a one-to-one basis (and so be analogous to co-therapy) or in a group. The normal arrangement in peer supervision is that two or more therapists agree to meet for supervision and to share the time for the presentation of case work between them. Each member of the peer supervision set acts as a supervisor to the other(s).

Though there are advantages to this form of supervision at least as an addition to more formal supervision, it may not offer the same developmental opportunities as individual supervision or group supervision and it should be approached with caution. The professional organisations seem to have a somewhat wary attitude to peer supervision and are likely to view it only as appropriate to experienced therapists. I think that this is because there are fears that in this situation a collusive relationship might develop and that, for beginning therapists, it is less suitable because the voice of experience and detachment may be missing. Certainly, I know of a number of therapists who have fallen foul of professional codes more by accident than design and whose major form of supervision was in a peer group. There is at least the suggestion that the mistakes they made would not have occurred if they had had a more formal arrangement for supervision. Feltham and Dryden (1994: 48) point out that in peer supervision, nobody has the clear responsibility to take action about any unprofessional behaviour, confrontation may be avoided and the quality of supervision may be restricted by lack of skills, experience and expertise. Hawkins and Shohet (1989: 105) also consider the traps into which peer groups may fall.

Advantages of peer supervision include that it is likely to be more or less cost free and that (because it is a relationship of equals) the power issue which may be present in other supervisory arrangements is less likely to arise. Between peers there may be a greater understanding of developmental needs and a sharing of the support function of supervision. Feltham and Dryden (1994: 48) write that peer supervision may be the form of supervision of choice for very experienced therapists. Certainly, a well-constructed peer supervision group with a system for attending to their own group dynamics (for example occasional input from an external moderator or facilitator) does offer developmental opportunities to more experienced therapists. The support of peers who may be experiencing similar processes is of great value, as is the sharing of experience. Hawkins and Shohet (1989: 106–107) offer advice about forming peer supervision groups and organising peer supervision meetings and this is a useful starting point for any group of therapists wishing to constitute such a group. Their advice is given in Box 5.4.

Self-supervision

Although it can never replace properly constituted individual or group supervision, there are developmental opportunities in self-supervision. Reflecting on thoughts, feelings and actions in response to client behaviour and material is useful in terms of

---

Box 5.4 Advice about peer supervision groups

- Choose group members who share values but take different approaches to client work.
- Limit group size to no more than seven people.
- Be clear about commitment.
- Clearly contract for frequency and place of meetings, time boundaries, confidentiality, how time will be allocated and how the process of the group will be managed.
- Be clear about the different expectations of group members.
- Be clear about organisational responsibilities.
- In each session, allow time for feedback.
- Hold regular review sessions (Hawkins and Shohet suggest three-monthly).

---

development and may be deepened by writing case notes, which Hawkins and Shohet (1989: 28) say should record 'not only the facts necessary for professional practice, but reflects on the processes of the work and monitors our own body sensations, breathing, feelings, thoughts and actions, whilst with the client'. The use of audio and video tapes may contribute still further to this process.

Using supervision to clarify a programme of personal and professional development

Whatever form of supervision is used to support the therapist's case work, it may also be (with the consent of the supervisor and/ or group members) a place to consider developmental needs and ways in which these may be addressed. Sometimes through case presentation a need for the enhancement of skills or knowledge may become apparent and it is quite legitimate to use supervision to look at how this need may be met. Sometimes the needs are those of the therapist rather than the therapist in relation to individual clients. Perhaps a change in working practices, type of client or orientation is being considered or the therapist has a sense that some personal work might be helpful. All these and more are legitimate concerns to bring to supervision.

Therapists wishing to use supervision as a focus for determining (and perhaps meeting) their developmental needs might like to consider building a regular review element into the supervisory process. This review might comprise a self-assessment, an exploration of the needs, desires and ambitions of the therapist and some consideration of how these might be achieved. The role of the supervisor or group would be to facilitate this process and to offer feedback to the supervisee. I have found this really useful. It has been by looking at myself in relation to my client work in supervision that I have made some of the important discoveries and changes in my professional career. Sometimes I have found that I was more jaded and in need of refreshment than I had realised, sometimes I have recognised that my interests were carrying me in new directions and sometimes I have gained some measure of my ignorance! With the discovery, and through further consideration with my supervisor, has come some clarification, some sense of how to proceed. This has been invaluable and fundamental to my development.

Sometimes the process of review 'just happens'. It is the natural result of the therapist's stage of development or a response to a particular client or type of client. Sometimes it can be more structured. There are many advantages for using the part or the whole of a supervision session for this purpose and on a regular basis (how often will vary with the therapist and the stage of development of that therapist). Some of the questions to pose in such a review are included in those suggested in Chapter 2 as a means of assessing current knowledge and practice (see p. 36).

Developing as a supervisor

For many counsellors, becoming a supervisor is a natural developmental step. It is a progression which acknowledges experience and expertise and which offers an extension to their repertoire. Experienced counsellors who have acquired a reputation for professionalism and competence may find that they are asked for supervision by less experienced or trainee therapists. Alternatively, they may decide that they now know enough to put themselves forward in the capacity of supervisor. However, it is important to realise that experience and expertise as a counselling practitioner do not necessarily mean competence and ability as a supervisor. Clarkson and Gilbert (1991: 143) agree with this statement and write that supervision should not necessarily be seen as a career progression for counsellors. In their view, good supervisors need to be aware of what they are doing and why and to 'convey it clearly and effectively'. Hawkins and Shohet (1989: 33–40) write about becoming a supervisor. They consider the question 'Why be a supervisor?', the qualities needed to be a good supervisor and supervisors' roles.

Supervisors sometimes still simply rise from the ranks of practitioners, having learned their skills from years of experience in the field and from being themselves supervisees. This is a time-honoured practice and Hawkins and Shohet (1989: 33) consider that it is unreasonable to expect to give good supervision to others without first learning how to be a good supervisee. However, would-be supervisors also opt for training in the skills of supervision.

There is a growing number of training courses for supervisors and these courses adopt a variety of models. These include psychodynamic and person centred approaches but the importance of creative approaches and therapies offering brief or more structured interventions is becoming more evident in courses for supervisors. Training in supervision is offered in both the academic and the private sector and courses are commonly advertised in the counselling press. The courses offering a qualification in supervision normally require participants to be practising as supervisors at least in the later stages of training. A course of training in supervision offers not only a theoretical framework for the practice of supervision but also the occasion to meet and interact with others acting as supervisors. This provides an opportunity for support and the exchange of ideas.

In addition to (or perhaps as an alternative to) formal training, a would-be supervisor could include a programme of 'self-improvement' (see Box 5.5).

Accreditation of supervisors

In 1988 the BAC introduced a scheme leading to the accreditation of supervisors of counselling practice. This was a process of peer assessment. In 1995 this scheme was updated and (so that it was consistent with the scheme for practitioners) renamed as the accreditation of supervisors.

Accredited supervisors are accredited members of the BAC (or are trained and experienced to the same standard) who have demonstrated that they are both experienced practitioners and supervisors. They are trained in supervision either by successfully

---

Box 5.5   A programme of 'self-improvement' for would-be supervisors

- extensive reading about supervision (Hawkins and Shohet, 1989; Feltham and Dryden, 1994 and Page and Wosket, 1994 are places to start);
- attendance at short courses offering particular approaches to supervision: those currently on offer include, for instance, the use of creative techniques, the use of psychosynthesis and the use of cognitive approaches;
- varying the style of supervision received, perhaps joining a supervision group or receiving supervision from a supervisor with different skills and orientation;
- increasing the range of clients encountered and the nature of clinical practice.

Each of these will contribute to the skills and knowledge the supervisor is able to bring to the supervisory session and thus to the service of the supervisee and the supervisee's clients.

---

completing an appropriate course (see Box 5.6 for a representative selection of such courses) or by training with an experienced supervisor. Accredited supervisors have had at least 100 hours' experience of supervision over a period of not less than two years with a minimum of four individual supervisees and one group. This work must itself have been supervised.

The process of accreditation as a supervisor shares something with the process of personal accreditation in that applicants are asked to write about their philosophy and to provide a transcript of a supervision session. This material is considered by an assessor of the applicant's choice prior to attendance at a recognition day when the applicant is required to present a piece of current counselling work for another candidate to supervise and themselves to supervise a similar piece of work. This is followed by an interview with the assessors. Again, like individual accreditation, the assessors are looking for congruence and coherence between what the applicant says they do, the evidence from an actual supervision session and the applicant's performance at the accreditation event.

This procedure can be very stressful (for many people, peer review is exceptionally challenging) but if the applicant pays close attention to the criteria and guidelines *and* takes note of the advice of a consultant and/or the first assessor, failure is less

Box 5.6 Some courses in supervision

This list of courses is representative of those widely advertised in 1995.
It is not comprehensive and the inclusion of a course on this list is not
in itself a recommendation. Equally, courses other than those appearing
in this list may be as good as those which do.

Cascade Training Associates: 42 Holland Street, Brighton, BN2 2WB.
Counselling Supervisor Training

Metanoia: 13 North Common Road, Ealing, London, W5 2QB
Diploma in Supervision

Minster Centre: 1 Drakes Court Yard, 291, Kilburn High Road, London,
  NW6 7JR
Certificate in Integrative Supervision (1 year), Diploma in Integrative
Supervision (2 years)

Oxford School of Psychotherapy and Counselling Ltd.: 193 Cowley
  Road, Oxford, OX4 1UT
Diploma in Counselling Supervision

Person Centred Therapy (Britain): 23 Spring Gardens, Edinburgh, EH8
  8HU
Certificate in Person Centred Counselling Supervision

Stockton Centre for Psychotherapy and Counselling: 77 Acklam Road,
  Thornaby on Tees, Cleveland, TS17 7BD
Certificate in the Practice of Supervision

University of Birmingham, School of Continuing Studies: Edgbaston,
  Birmingham, B15 2TT
Advanced Certificate in Supervision

University of Keele, Department of Applied Social Studies: Keele,
  Staffordshire, ST5 5BG
Certificate in Supervision

University of Manchester, Department of Extra Mural Studies:
  Manchester, M13 9PL
Certificate in the Supervision of Counselling and Therapy

University College of Ripon and York St John, Counselling and
  Consultancy Unit: Lord Mayor's Walk, York YO3 7EX
Certificate in Supervision

WPF Counselling: 23 Kensington Square, London W8 5HN
Diploma in Supervision

likely. Feltham and Dryden (1994: 121) write that though the processes of accreditation and recognition (which accreditation of supervisors replaced) are often thought of as rather negative, bureaucratic procedures, they have the great value of validating the skills the applicant has and of exposing them to new ways of looking at their work. In an interview with Stephen Palmer (1995a: 28), Brenda Clowes (a BAC-recognised supervisor) spoke of the worries she had about exposing herself to the recognition process and of the great value of consulting someone who was already a recognised supervisor about that process. Her advice to any prospective applicant for recognition as a supervisor is to have a session with someone who has successfully completed the process. In this session, Clowes suggests discussing the prospective applicant's work, whether they meet the criteria for recognition, what to expect on the recognition day and how to go about making an application. She also says that the effects of becoming a recognised supervisor included increases in her confidence and her business.

Summary

Professional organisations require practising therapists to be in supervision. This serves several functions. All of these functions relate to professional development but (in this respect) the 'formative' function is most important.

The developmental needs from supervision vary with experience. With respect to these needs, issues to consider in selecting a supervisor include the orientation, training and experience of the supervisor and the style of supervision (individual, group or peer).

The developmental aspects of supervision are highly valued by therapists but individual supervision has some limitations. These limitations may be addressed through other forms of supervision.

Group supervision offers the supervisee access to wider variety of expertise, experience and opinion than does individual supervision. It allows group members to creatively explore the therapeutic relationship.

Group supervision also has its drawbacks: there is less time for each group member to present their own client material, and the dynamics of the group may become a complicating factor.

Peer supervision is an alternative to individual and group supervision. This has some advantages but may not offer the same developmental opportunities. Professional organisations are likely to view this form of supervision as most appropriate to experienced therapists.

Supervision may be used to clarify a programme of professional and personal development. This may be done through regular review, which (facilitated by the supervisor or the group) might comprise a self-assessment, an exploration of the needs, desires and ambitions of the therapist and some consideration of how these might be achieved.

Becoming a supervisor may itself be a developmental stage for some therapists. There are a number of training courses available for people who wish to make this move. Programmes of 'self-improvement' – including extensive reading about supervision, attending workshops or short courses addressing aspects of supervision, and varying the style of supervision received – may be appropriate for developing supervisors.

The BAC offers a scheme for the accreditation of supervisors. To be eligible for accreditation, supervisors must be able to demonstrate that they have training and experience in supervision.

6

Contributing to the Furtherance of Knowledge

Perhaps the idea of contributing to the furtherance of knowledge about counselling and psychotherapy sounds awe-inspiring, pretentious or just plain dull, but without it therapy wouldn't exist at all. It is by the continual efforts of practitioners to communicate their ideas and discoveries that counselling and psychotherapy are kept alive, vibrant and vital. Without these efforts the profession would stagnate and die. The great innovators of the psychotherapeutic movement were, through their books, papers and teaching, contributing to the furtherance of knowledge but so is the therapist who puts on a workshop for colleagues. It isn't necessary to be a Freud, Rogers, Assagioli or Lazarus to contribute to what is known about therapy: it is something that is open to us all. When any of us communicate the results of our experiential learning to our peers we are engaged in contributing to the furtherance of knowledge. Similarly, when we publicly speculate about process and outcome in therapy and engage in discussion and debate with colleagues, we are furthering our own knowledge and facilitating the increased knowledge of others. More obviously, teaching and the educative aspects of supervision constitute contributions to the furtherance of knowledge.

Within the profession, contributing to the furtherance of knowledge is a fairly ordinary, often informal process but it can also be more formal and systematic. It is those more formal and systematic activities (including running a workshop, writing for publication and conducting research) which may be considered part of continuing professional development. Even these may be far less daunting than they at first seem, and this chapter offers some ideas and advice on how to set about the task of making a formal contribution.

Running a workshop

Workshops tend to address the acquisition of skills, the demonstration of technique or to be experiential (that is, they offer a chance to experience the technique or approach rather than to be told about it) but a facilitated debate or discussion might also constitute a workshop. They are a way for practitioners to convey to others something they know about a certain way of working, their experience with a particular client group or their knowledge about a specific issue. Workshops may be experiential (i.e. involving all the participants in some activity), they may involve the presenter(s) in demonstrating a technique or they may take the form of a presentation of ideas, observations and speculations. Because it is usually less formal than the presentation of a paper or the delivery of a lecture and because the emphasis is most often on the practical, the workshop format provides an ideal way for many practitioners to communicate their knowledge or their skills. Though the primary aim in running a workshop may be the dissemination of knowledge, it is also a good way of soliciting feedback and gaining access to the ideas of the participants. I have found that in addition to the learning I achieve in the preparation of a workshop (and I always find out something), I invariably learn something from the participants. Sometimes this learning takes the form of a contribution from the knowledge of a member of the group, sometimes it results from the process within the workshop, but it is always there.

If you are experienced in a particular way of working or with a particular client group and you wish others to know more about your field or you have a sense that there is a thirst or need for this knowledge, then a workshop provides a possible outlet. Workshops can take many forms, addressing any of several issues. I have co-ordinated several series of workshops for therapists, including workshops with the following titles:

- Working with suicidal clients
- Introduction to dramatherapy

- Creative approaches to supervision
- Working with adults sexually abused as children
- Gay and lesbian bereavement
- Psychosynthesis
- Shame: working with men
- Person centred expressive therapy
- Issues of race and culture in counselling

This is a diverse range of topics yet each workshop was presented in the same context and occupied the same time slot though the style and objectives of the presenters varied. The workshop is a very flexible form and can be adapted to most issues in counselling.

If you have expertise or knowledge, you may find that you are invited by counselling trainers or groups of practitioners to give a workshop (see the guidelines in Box 6.1). If you are lucky, you may even be offered a fee and certainly the organisers will take care of the venue, publicity and bookings. If you decide that you have something you want to communicate in this form but lack such an invitation, you have to find a way of delivering your workshop. There are several possibilities.

Each year, the professional organisations which offer training conferences actively invite applications to run workshops. These requests are usually made through the counselling and psychotherapy journals. The organisers of international conferences extend similar invitations. Anyone wishing to offer a workshop which is relevant to the aims of the conference organisers and likely to be of interest to conference participants may very well receive a positive response to an application to do so.

If an application is accepted, then the workshop facilitator may be eligible for a reduced fee for the conference and/or payment for the workshop (this is less likely to be true of the smaller organisations). Training conferences often have themes, and workshops which address an aspect of the theme or are related to it are more likely to be accepted than those which do not. At any conference, there are workshops which have at best a tenuous link to the theme, so if you have a good idea, it may be worth applying anyway. Giving a workshop at an annual conference may sound daunting but there is great potential for support. There will be many other workshop presenters with whom to share experiences and conference organisers usually work very hard to

Box 6.1   Guidelines for running a workshop

- Pick a subject or issue in which you have a genuine interest, expertise and knowledge.

- Be familiar with the material you intend to present and/or the structure you intend to use. A dry run may be helpful.

- In your promotional material, make a very clear statement about the content of the workshop, your expertise and training and any expectations you have of participants.

- In your planning, decide how many participants you are prepared to accept on the workshop (do you have a maximum or a minimum?), what sort of equipment you need and what you require of the space in which the workshop will be held.

- Think about the structure of your workshop. Be aware of the parameters of time, and work within them. Plan to the degree that suits your nature and the nature of the workshop. Although it may be tempting to fill all the time with the presentation, remember to allow time for questions, feedback and sharing from the participants. Workshop participants tend to like to have their say and their reaction provides useful material for the refinement of future presentations.

- In your workshop, always allow for the unexpected. It tends to happen – especially in experiential workshops. Always have a contingency plan. Knowing that the pattern of your design may be interrupted or disrupted and/or having an alternative course of action helps you deal with any disruption when it happens.

- Consider how at the end of the workshop you will form a view of how successful it has been. You might like to prepare a question-naire for the participants to complete (if you do this, you will get a better response if you ask that it is done *before* they leave, but then they may be less objective). You may have specific questions you want answered in the workshop or you may just invite any response that participants choose to offer. However you do it (even in private and afterwards), an active consideration of what was good, what was less good, what worked, what didn't work, what was missing, etc. is important to the process of development and to the structure and success of future workshops.

- After the workshop, make some provision for debriefing and pro-cessing. Especially if your workshop has been experiential, you might like to make some provision for 'supervision', going over what happened with a colleague. This is a separate process from the consideration of feedback for it involves the personal rather than the professional.

- Use all of the above to help plan your next workshop!

ensure that the needs of facilitators are met. Also, it is important to realise that even in large events, facilitators have control over their workshops. For instance, in an application to run a workshop potential facilitators are usually asked to specify a maximum number of participants and to make a request for any equipment they require.

If you are seeking an alternative to presentation at a large event and haven't been invited to give a workshop, an alternative is self-promotion. You may approach bodies you know to co-ordinate programmes of counselling workshops, and make your offer. It is sensible to be explicit about the content of your proposed workshop: state for whom you think it might be suitable, the reason why you are offering the workshop and your authority to do so (i.e. your expertise, experience and training). Sometimes this works, but series of workshops may be organised a year or longer in advance so you may have a long wait before you get to make your contribution. Another approach is to act independently. If you are relatively certain of the need for and interest in the workshop you wish to offer, an option would be to organise, advertise and recruit to the workshop yourself.

How and why to get 'specialist expertise'

The above section on running a workshop and the next section on writing for publication are predicated on the assumption that the facilitator or writer has something new or interesting to contribute or is privy to some less well-known skill, technique or mode of practice. This raises the question as to how practitioners may acquire such specialist expertise and perhaps why they should bother. Like so many questions raised by the whole process of continuing development, there are no universal answers but there *are* some general trends. Broadly speaking, specialist expertise comes from:

1. *Experience*: Perhaps working with a particular client group over time allows a reflective practitioner to reach some conclusions about therapist behaviours which are valued by those clients. Very experienced practitioners may be able to make valuable observations about trends in client work (for example have there been ethnographic changes in the users of counselling? Do clients for whom counselling was apparently

effective eventually re-refer?) and to offer a view of counsellor development based on their experience of themselves and of colleagues.

2. *Training*: Counsellors who train in an approach to therapy or to a client group which is not well known to their colleagues (perhaps because it is new, perhaps because it is most practised elsewhere) may have opportunities to introduce their new skills to others even quite shortly after they qualify. This could take the form of introductory workshops or papers about the approach in practice.

3. *Research*: Counsellors with a curiosity about issues of theory and practice who investigate those issues in a systematic way (see the section on research, pp. 111–120) are likely to acquire 'specialist' knowledge – at least in the sense that they will know something 'new'. This knowledge may have value to other practitioners.

4. *Novel ideas and innovations*: Every approach to therapy, every counselling technique, was thought up by somebody. Sometimes what was new was a modification of or a reaction to something pre-existing (for example, humanistic approaches are commonly thought to have resulted from a dissatisfaction with and reaction to psychodynamic and behavioural approaches). Sometimes what was new was the result of a fusion of different approaches or the introduction of some strategy from outside the field of counselling to therapeutic practice. There are many examples of the latter approach and some are mentioned in this book (see, for example, Bettelheim, 1976; Rogers, 1985; Bolton, 1995; Knights, 1995; Wilkins, 1995). Novel ideas are fuelled by experience and curiosity: they stem from a 'what if?' attitude. *What* will happen *if* I get my supervisees to show me how their clients behave? *What* might be useful to my clients *if* I apply my knowledge of Buddhism to my counselling practice? Of course novel ideas are not likely to lead to a reputation for specialist expertise unless they actually result in useful practices!

The above gives some indication of how specialist knowledge and expertise might be acquired but doesn't indicate why this might be worthwhile. Advantages of specialist expertise might be (for those who want it) increased prestige and status, the referral to the practitioner of clients for whom this expertise is seen as relevant, opportunities to disseminate this expertise and (because of one or more of these) the possibility of increased income – authority and rarity command a price in today's market economy.

Writing for publication

> Publishing is almost always likely to enhance your reputation and career as well as being intrinsically satisfying. No one will know what brilliant ideas you have unless you publicise them! (Colin Feltham, personal communication, 1995)

Another way for practitioners to offer the fruits of their knowledge and experience to the profession as a whole is to write for publication. This need not be an intimidating prospect nor need a written contribution take the form of a lengthy treatise or an exposition of the results of a piece of research. Written contributions can take many forms. At one end of the spectrum writing might take the form of a book while at the other might be 'letters to the editor', with journal articles falling somewhere between. Writing a book is a challenging task and although it might be the best way of making public a particular (and relatively large) body of knowledge, it is probably advisable to start with shorter pieces of writing. Writing a letter to the editor (for those journals that have them) may be a good way of dipping a toe into the process of committing ideas and opinions to print. It is certainly a good way of making a concise point, responding to the views of another writer or contributing to a debate.

Another way to make a written contribution may be to write a review of a book, though unsolicited reviews are unlikely to be published. However, many journals include book reviews and the review editors are often looking for more reviewers. *Counselling* for instance publishes not only book reviews but a list of all the other books received by the reviews editor and an invitation for readers who wish to join the panel of reviewers to write to him expressing their interest. Reviewing a book offers the developmental opportunities arising from reading it, the experience of writing (and often concisely) *and* it is normal practice for reviewers to keep the books as compensation for their efforts.

Writing and submitting a journal article

For most therapists with something to say in print, the most appropriate outlet is in the form of an article or paper for a journal. This provides a way of conveying ideas, experiences, discoveries or opinions at moderate length (usually 2,000 to 6,000 words) and in a way which makes the contribution accessible to an appropriate readership.

There are many outlets for articles about therapy and there is space for contributions of many kinds. There are academic journals (such as the *British Journal of Guidance and Counselling*) which are seen primarily as an outlet for papers which relay research findings or those in which contributions to theoretical understanding are made. Professional journals (such as *Counselling*) are perceived to have a broader remit and to publish papers dealing with accounts of practice and the experiences of practitioners as well as papers of the type which might appear in academic journals. Professional journals are often associated with specific organisations (for instance *Counselling* is the journal of the BAC) but most of them will accept contributions from non-members if they are relevant and of the required standard. In addition to journals addressing the broad spectrum of therapy, there are more specialist journals publishing articles about a particular orientation (e.g. *Transactional Analysis Journal* or *Person Centred Practice*) the editors of which will probably show interest in any contribution which adds to the knowledge of the theory and/or practice of the relevant approach. The best way to understand the distinct areas of interest represented by different journals and to get some sense of the articles which are likely to interest their editors is to actually read them! In this way, a potential writer will gain an idea of the standard of writing and content expected of contributions, the subject area of the journal as well as the style of writing expected.

Stages in the process of getting a paper published

> The Features Editor welcomes – research findings, counselling practice demonstrated through descriptions of case studies or group sessions, etc., theoretical studies, considered responses to published articles or current issues, reports of experiments. (from Information for Contributors, *Counselling*)

The first stage in the preparation of an article or paper is to decide what is to be written about. This may be an anecdotal account of work with particular clients or in a particular context, a contribution to the debate about ethics, a report of research findings, the description of a technique, a comparative study of ways of practising as a therapist or anything else about which the writer has an opinion, knowledge or experience. As the idea takes shape, it is advisable to check that what you wish to write about, what you think is new, exciting and a useful contribution hasn't already appeared in print. This is most relevant if you are reporting research findings (but a literature search should precede the research itself) or describing a technique when it is possible that someone will have had the same idea and got there first.

Whatever the content of the paper might be, a second – and vital – stage is to decide on the likely audience. Who you are writing for may very well influence how you write. The language and style appropriate to addressing a specialist audience (e.g. therapists of a particular orientation) might not be appropriate to a more general readership. At this stage it is also worth considering likely outlets for the finished product. Every journal has a house style: a form in which the editor prefers papers to be written. This will include a preferred structure, a specified length and possibly a view about the use of non-sexist language. If you hope to be published in *Counselling*, it is sensible to write in a style compatible with the articles that appear in that journal. If you were writing with a view to being published in *Psychotherapy* a different style and different language might be appropriate, though the principal ideas might be the same.

When you have made up your mind to which journal you will submit your finished article, make sure that you know in what form the editor requires submissions. Most journals include 'Information for Contributors' in every issue; this is often to be found on one of the inside covers. This information will include precise instructions about the form a manuscript must take (usually typed, double-spaced and multiple copies), the maximum length of an acceptable article and perhaps an indication of the requirements with respect to client anonymity or the use of language. Some things (like the way authors are cited in the text and references given) may not be made explicit in these instructions. For these you will have to look at the articles themselves. It saves a lot of time and trouble if your contribution reaches the editor in the desired format – indeed if it doesn't, it *may* be rejected out of hand. It makes sense to write in the appropriate style from the outset.

When you have decided upon the content and the style, the third stage is to do the actual writing. For some writers, the only way is to start at the beginning and continue to the end. For others, it is the middle that dictates the nature of the start and finish of their paper and so it is sensible to start there. Some people like to make a plan, to map out a structure and to work to headings. It doesn't really matter *how* you set about your writing as long as the finished product is understandable and conveys what you wish. What matters is that you find a way that suits you and that enables you to set forth your ideas. What seems to be important is that writers write what they can when they can. Writing for publication is rarely smooth. Writer's block is a real phenomenon encountered at some time by most, if not all, writers and it takes a variety of forms. The best advice I have received for overcoming such blocks is simply to sit and write whatever I can. It is better to start in the middle of something than to struggle for ages with the right way to begin. The appropriate beginning may very well become apparent later and, certainly, there is something about the process of writing which facilitates more writing.

Once you have set down your ideas in writing, the process of refinement follows. It is unlikely that you will be perfectly satisfied with your first draft and in any case reading through what you have written is very helpful in refining what you have to say and how you say it. If you have one, word-processing programs for personal computers offer a way of checking spelling and some-times sentence construction as well. This can be useful. I find it very helpful to get a friend or colleague to read through my writing. They so often spot the obvious mistakes I have missed and also offer valuable feedback about the clarity and content of my writing. I find the advice of readers who aren't counsellors particularly helpful. The final task before submitting the article to a journal is to incorporate the revisions and additions which have been suggested.

Submitting a paper to a professional or academic journal, even in the right form, does not guarantee its acceptance for publica-tion. While there may be some differences between editors and between journals, what happens to a paper on its receipt is broadly similar wherever it is sent. In the first instance, receiving editors check that the paper is in an acceptable form and make a decision about the appropriateness of it for their journals. A paper may be refused at this stage. If an editor thinks that the paper is likely to be suitable and is interested in publishing it, the paper is sent anonymously to two or more referees. This is why editors require more than one copy of any submitted paper. These referees (who are normally experienced practitioners and writers themselves) read the article (the double spacing makes this easier and allows them to write notes in the text if that is helpful). This reading is with a critical eye. The task of the referee is to form a judgement about the ideas given expression in the article and to offer feedback about its content and construction; they may also offer an opinion about the acceptability of the paper for publication.

Referees return their comments to editors, who use them to inform their judgement about the acceptability of the paper. The views, comments and suggestions of the referees will usually be conveyed to the writer of the paper but in such a way as to protect the anonymity of the referees. This process of ensuring that the referees do not know who the author of a paper is and that the author does not know who the referees are is seen as a way of guaranteeing objectivity. Sometimes, as a result of this, editors refuse a paper for publication (they will nearly always offer their reasons). A paper is rarely accepted in exactly the form in which it is submitted: most commonly, editors offer a conditional acceptance. These conditions are usually based on the feedback from the referees. It might be that they have made suggestions or asked questions about the material presented in the paper, or it might be that some things are unclear. Whatever the case, along with a conditional acceptance will come a definite indication as to what changes might make a paper acceptable.

For some writers, particularly if it is their first effort, having a paper returned after a critical appraisal in which it is found wanting can be hurtful. This isn't the intention. Anonymous reviewing (besides being a way of protecting standards) is meant to be constructive. The task of the editor and the referees is to work with writers to ensure that they give the best account of themselves and present their contributions in the best way. Any feedback or criticism offered to a writer is intended to inform the process of rewriting or future writing.

If your article is returned but the editor indicates that it may (or will) be acceptable if it is modified or changed in some way then you are faced with a choice. If you agree with the criticisms and suggestions, it may simply be that you rewrite your piece accordingly and offer the revision to the same journal. If the revisions asked for are relatively minor and can be seen by the editor to be included or countered in some legitimate way, then the likelihood is that the paper will be accepted at this stage. If the revisions suggested amount to major rewriting, the paper will be sent once more to the referees and the whole process will be repeated.

If you disagree with some or all the comments and criticisms you have been offered and feel that to incorporate any suggested changes would obscure rather than clarify your message, then you have a choice. You could re-submit your paper, explaining why you disagree (and perhaps offering evidence for your view) or you could submit your paper to a different journal. Editors and referees (and I write as both) are not perfect. They make mistakes and sometimes misunderstand. It may be appropriate to question the criticisms offered: sometimes another editor and other referees will take a different view of the same paper (I have the experience of having a paper refused by a British journal and welcomed unaltered by a more prestigious American journal) but usually it is worth taking note of the feedback. Certainly I advise careful reconsideration of such feedback after allowing time following its initial receipt.

If all goes well and your paper is accepted, it will eventually appear in print. This can be some time after you first submitted your paper and perhaps a year or more following the final acceptance. When it does appear, some journals will offer you copies of the whole journal (e.g. six copies of *Counselling* are sent to contributors) or reprints of your paper (fifty in the case of the *British Journal of Guidance and Counselling*) and some merely the honour of being published. Although it can be a long and sometimes painful process, writing for publication does bring rewards and it is certainly a developmental exercise.

Writing a book

Writing a book is a major project and not one to be undertaken lightly. Even a short book is likely to be at least five to ten times the length of a journal article. Whereas journal editors welcome and depend upon unsolicited articles, book publishers tend to take a different view. For the most part, they seem to prefer commissioning work or at the very least to become involved in the planning stages of a projected book. That said, there is a burgeoning of books in the field of counselling and psychotherapy and the therapist with a particular expertise or who has identified a gap in the market *and* who has proven ability to write may find that a publisher is interested in a proposal for a book.

If you choose this route (and it might be a good idea to seek the advice of someone who has already written a book before you do), the starting point is to identify one or more publishers who might be interested in publishing a book of the kind you envisage. A look along the shelves of a library or a bookshop will give you some indication as to which publishing houses offer books dealing with similar subjects. The next stage is to write to your chosen publisher with your proposal. This should include an outline of the content of your proposed book, perhaps giving a synopsis of each chapter, its likely readership, an indication of any similar works, the new contributions or perspectives your book will offer and evidence of your ability to write and of your knowledge of the subject area. It may also be a good idea to indicate by when you would expect to complete your work (which probably is later than you first thought). If your proposal seems relevant to the publisher's list and to have the potential to sell, the publisher will often send it to reviewers (who have knowledge of the area and the existing literature). If these reviewers favour the proposal the publisher is likely to express interest and if further negotiations are successfully completed, you may ultimately be offered a contract to write the book you envisaged. You may even receive an advance against future royalties.

Co-authoring and editing

Writing a book can be a collaborative endeavour. Sometimes two or more writers become joint authors – that is they all take responsibility for the text as a whole. If you choose this route, then your relationship with a publisher is broadly similar to that of a single author but you should give careful consideration to how you and your co-author(s) will work. It is advisable to agree before pen is put to paper (or fingers to keyboard!) exactly what your separate responsibilities will be. Some of the things you might like to consider are:

- Who will write what?
- How will it be written?

- What will be your timetable?
- How will information, work-in-progress, etc. be shared?
- What will be the process of review?
- Who will do the rewriting?
- How will you resolve any disagreement?
- How will royalties be apportioned?

The convention for jointly authored work is that the names of authors appear in alphabetical order unless there is some reason for this to be otherwise.

Being the editor of a book or a series is a rather different proposition. The task of the editor does not involve originating written material (although editors often contribute chapters in the books they edit or books in the series) but the co-ordination of the efforts of others. Broadly speaking, an editor collates contributions, ensures that they are in the form required and offers constructive criticism, ideas and support to the writers. Editors may have the task of recruiting contributors or this may be pre-determined (as in, for instance, a volume of conference proceedings).

If you have an idea for an edited volume and who may be invited to contribute to it, then publishers may be interested to consider your proposition. They are most likely to offer a contract to prospective editors who can demonstrate their abilities (perhaps because they are writers themselves or have previous experience of editing) and who can be convincing not only about the idea but about the contributors. Publishers are likely to want to know that the contributors being suggested really are ready, willing and able to provide a chapter!

Contributing to the advancement of the understanding of the theory and practice of counselling by research

> Good research should, ultimately, allow the development of a better understanding of events and processes that are experienced by individual counsellors and clients, and therefore enable practitioners to learn from each other. (McLeod, 1993: 176)

> Evaluation and research activities arouse strong feeling in counsellors, more so than in clients. (Shipton, 1994: 38)

For a long time and notwithstanding the contributions of Rogers and his colleagues in the middle of the century and later researchers, an anti-research stance seems to have been prevalent amongst practitioners. Hicks and Wheeler (1994: 29) reflect this when they write:

> For some counsellors the whole issue of research with its connotations of experimentation and quantification is seen as being incompatible with the process of counselling and for that reason alone it is eschewed.

This anti-research stance appears to come from a perceived contradiction between working with and being interested in people and their processes, behaviour or thinking (i.e. being a practitioner) and the translation of the therapeutic endeavour into facts, figures, measures of effectiveness and statements about outcome (i.e. being a researcher). Somehow, in many minds research and practice are seen as, if not unrelated, then the provinces of different people. Research is the province of *men* in white coats who lack compassion and see people as objects. Practitioners on the other hand are genuinely interested in people and their experiences and are more interested in the quality of the therapeutic encounter than in its reduction to statistics! Linked to this perception of research as in some way dehumanising seems to be a belief that research is solely concerned with measures of effectiveness and with outcome and that these are of limited relevance to the process and value of therapy. Lynch (1996: 144–148) writing about the philosophical bases for counselling research, states that 'a piece of research should possess *internal consistency*'. For me, this includes the notion that counselling research could and should be conducted in a manner consistent with the philosophy *and practice* of the practitioner/researcher.

Of course evidence of the effectiveness of therapy is sought and it is especially important to the people who are paying the therapist for they are interested in *cost-effectiveness* (another source of resentment and tension?). Outcome too is important. In 1995 a special edition of *Changes* was devoted to the issue of outcome in psychotherapy. But these are not the only possibilities for research in therapy. Others include testing the validity and applications of theory, the monitoring of the therapist's own work, discovering the answer to particular questions, the development of new techniques and wider applications of therapy, investigations into the needs of particular client groups, comparing and contrasting approaches and many, many more. Just as research in therapy is not confined to demonstrations of its effectiveness, so its techniques are not only those of the laboratory and the statistician. The quantitative methods which loom large in the popular conception of research do have a place in *some* counselling research but qualitative methods (those which, for instance, deal with the subjective interpretations of the people involved in the research and which may incorporate the 'clients' as co-researchers) are and have been of increasing importance. Even in the field of outcome research this is true. McLeod (1995: 198) writes:

> It is also important that counsellors give themselves permission to engage in outcome research consistent with their distinctive needs and purposes.

Kate Kirk, a practising therapist and researcher, refers to the widespread perception of research amongst practitioners as 'the Research Monster', some sort of malign creature that interferes with or even prevents real therapeutic work (personal communication). This monster is the manifestation of the anxieties, fears and fantasies that practitioners have about research.

Kirk uses this image of research as a way of accessing these fears and fantasies and facilitating their expression. Having allowed this, her intention is to introduce people to some of the newer concepts in ways of research in therapy and to put the monster in perspective, for the truth is that research is a very ordinary activity.

Doing research is a natural act for human beings. When a baby puts an object in its mouth, it is conducting research. It is encountering and sensing the object and reaching conclusions about the object and itself in relation to it. Similarly, when a trainee practitioner first uses a newly acquired skill with a client and reflects upon the result, that is research. Likewise, writing a case study which involves reflecting on the use of skills and/or processes within the relationship involves research. Our development as reflective practitioners, though it has little to do with measurement, is the result of research and integrating the findings of that research. It is as we reflect upon our experiences and refine our practice as a result of these reflections that we develop as therapists. This is a form of research. McLeod (1994: 4) writes:

> A counselling session with a client can be seen as a piece of research, a piecing together of information and understanding, followed by testing the validity of conclusions and actions based on that shared knowing.

In this way, each therapist builds up a picture of the way different clients respond to different interventions, and of themselves in relation to their clients. Each of us develops a unique perspective, an individual way of understanding the process of therapy. One way in which practitioners can contribute to the understanding of counselling and psychotherapy is to formalise and make public the results of their experiences, reflections and experiments.

Increasingly, there is interest in the experiences clients have of the therapeutic relationship and the subjective experiences they and therapists have of processes within therapy. This is the province of qualitative research which makes use of 'new paradigms' (Reason and Rowan, 1981 provides a good source book for some of these). These new paradigms or models provide methods of enquiry different from the traditional logical positivistic research methods appropriate to science and are generally much more sympathetic to the ethos and purposes of therapy.

Although research is a fairly commonplace activity and there is a case for arguing that all therapists are researchers, research as professional development does require at least a degree of structure and formality. McLeod (1994: 4) offers the following 'useful working definition' of research:

> a systematic process of critical inquiry leading to valid propositions and conclusions that are communicated to interest others.

For research to be effective and of value to others, it must be conducted in a meaningful way which demonstrates its validity and therefore the authenticity of any findings or conclusions, and these findings and conclusions must be communicated to others in an understandable way. The research process is cyclical and each cycle takes the form of observation, reflection and experimentation. That is a process of starting with what is seen, thinking about what that might mean, what might be happening and then taking some action which might inform any tentative conclusion or provide information which seems to be missing. A very simple example of such a cycle might centre on a cup from which a steam-like vapour can be seen to be emerging:

- *Observation*: 'Steam' is seen to be emerging from the cup.
- *Reflection*: Something inside the cup is giving rise to the observed 'steam'. When vapour can be seen rising from a cup it (usually? may?) contain a hot liquid. If this is true the cup will feel warm or hot to the touch.
- *Experimentation*: Touch the cup.

This experiment results in another observation, i.e. a subjective estimation of the temperature of the contents of the cup. If the cup contains coffee, the cup will feel warm and, through further reflection, there will be some evidence for the tentative hypothesis that the cup contains a hot liquid. With this result, this piece of research might be at an end (except that there is no proof that the contents are liquid). Further experimentation to determine that the contents are liquid and the nature of the liquid would be a possible furtherance of this piece of research. If, on the other hand, it contained dry ice, then reflection will indicate that the tentative hypothesis falls.

Behind this piece of research lies one or more 'research questions'. In the above example, the question was, 'Does the cup contain a warm liquid?' Given the same observation, equally valid questions would have been 'What does the cup contain?' or 'Does the cup contain coffee?' Even in this relatively simple example, the same observation may lead to a number of research questions and each would require a different regime of reflection, experimentation and observation. Some research questions are broad ('What does the cup contain?'), some are focused ('Does the cup contain coffee?'). It is the research question which underpins the whole process and, in a way, it is the most important thing to get right. If, in my example, the real interest of the researcher is in whether the cup contains coffee and this question is precisely formulated, then many possible avenues of investigation (e.g. tests for orange juice, tea, dry ice) become unnecessary. Similar investigations which would lead to at best a partial answer (e.g. the cup contains a liquid) can be avoided. Get the question right and a great deal of time and energy can be saved.

While the answer to a research question can (and often does) lead to a second question and subsequent questions, the important starting point for any research is to reflect upon exactly what the researcher wishes to know. This precedes a consideration of how to find out for this would involve questions about methodology and ethics which are likely to depend upon the nature of the original question.

Doing a piece of research

> One of the chief sources of job satisfaction experienced by many counsellors is the sense of continually learning about human nature in response to the lives and personal worlds that clients allow them to enter. As part of this process, practitioners may find themselves with 'burning questions' that can only be answered by doing some research. (McLeod, 1994: 3)

McLeod considers that the process of research, the quest to answer a burning question, can be about the personal and professional development of the practitioner. The therapist with a well-formulated research question can, by following through the process implicit in the working definition of research given above, benefit both themselves and the profession as a whole. Research in therapy covers a multitude of approaches, questions and interpretations as a browse through the journals will demonstrate (*Counselling*, 6 (3) contains reports on the papers presented at the BAC research symposium, 1995 and provides an illustration of types of research and research issues). A small piece of research (e.g. what is the background of my clients?) can be undertaken cheaply and easily. More complex research (e.g. what techniques from dramatherapy do people who hear voices find to be useful?) will require more time and resources but, in a way, the processes are the same. For the practitioner considering embarking on a piece of research, there is really no substitute for reading the research literature and/or working with an experienced researcher, but the brief guide in Box 6.2 may be helpful.

Higher degrees by research

One of the possibilities for a practitioner wishing to undertake research is to register for a master's degree or a PhD with an institution of higher education. Both full-time and part-time routes are normally available and the time needed may range from one year full time for an MA by research to up to seven years (sometimes more) for a part-time PhD. Part-time routes tend to be cheaper than full-time routes and in any case may be most appropriate for practitioners whose research is based in their own practice.

Box 6.2   The research process

1. Formulate a research question. What do I want to know?

2. Refer to the literature. Is the answer to my question already known? What of relevance to my question is known? Who knows it and how did they find out? How might I answer my question?

3. What ethical issues are raised by my question and the way I propose to answer it? How may I resolve these issues?

4. In the light of the above, conduct the research, collect and process the data. This will involve at least one cycle through 'observation, reflection, experimentation' and probably more.

5. What have I discovered as the result of this process? Is it satisfactory? What new questions has this process thrown up? Do I need to answer them?

6. Present the research findings in such a way as to make them accessible to others (e.g. as a thesis, by writing for journals, giving a paper, running a workshop, as audio-visual aids).

Benefits of this way of doing research include that (if it is successful) it results in a qualification, the research will be supervised by one or more experienced researchers (who may also be practitioners), there will be access to library (see Boxes 6.3 and 6.4 for a guide to reading), to research seminars, computing and word-processing facilities and membership of a research community with whom to share feedback, doubts, fears and excitements. This can be very important, for a long piece of research may be experienced as at times lonely and dispiriting. Many universities also offer training in research methods to students registering for a higher degree and this can be an invaluable way of becoming acquainted with the variety of research techniques from which it is possible to select.

A practitioner considering undertaking a higher degree by research should approach potential supervisors with some indication of the issue in which they are interested. It is helpful if the potential supervisor has some acquaintance with at least the broad area of the researcher's interest but a supervisor's knowledge of the process and methodology of research may be even more beneficial. Potential supervisors are to be found in university departments offering qualifications in counselling and psychotherapy, psychology departments and social work departments. Some

Box 6.3 Suggested reading relevant to counselling research

GENERAL

Blaxter, L., Hughes, C. and Tight, M. (1996) *How to Research*. Buckingham: Open University Press.
This is a book for people who are new to research. It 'is about the practice and experience of doing research'.

Dryden, W. (ed.) (1996) *Research in Counselling and Psychotherapy*. London: Sage.
'This book bridges the gap that currently exists between research and practice in counselling and psychotherapy.' The authors make use of detailed clinical examples 'to demonstrate the practical relevance of research'.

McLeod, J. (1994) *Doing Counselling Research*. London: Sage.
A good introduction to research practices and issues relating to the study of counselling processes and outcomes. Readable, comprehensive and instructive.

QUALITATIVE AND 'NEW PARADIGM' RESEARCH

Denzin, N.K. and Lincoln, Y.S. (eds) (1994) *Handbook of Qualitative Research*. London: Sage.
A collection of papers addressing aspects of qualitative research.

Heron, J. (1996) *Co-operative Inquiry: Research into the Human Condition*. London: Sage.
A comprehensive overview of co-operative enquiry (a form of research in which the people who are being 'researched' are also contributing to the research process).

Miles, M. and Huberman, A. (1994) *Qualitative Data Analysis: A Sourcebook of New Methods*, 2nd edn. London: Sage.
Not specifically about counselling and psychotherapy but provides a range of different strategies that can be applied in qualitative data analysis.

Moustakas, C. (1994) *Phenomenological Research Methods*. London: Sage.
A step by step guide to the process of conducting a phenomenological study including 'form letters and other research tools to use in designing and conducting a study'.

Reason, P. and Rowan, J. (eds) (1981) *Human Inquiry: A Sourcebook of New Paradigm Research*. Chichester: Wiley.
Exactly what the title says it is. An important landmark in counselling research, setting out alternatives to the previously dominant logical-positivistic approaches.

QUANTITATIVE METHODS

Bausell, R.B. (1986) *A Practical Guide to Conducting Empirical Research.* New York: Harper & Row.

Bryman, A. and Cramer, D. (1990) *Quantitative Data Analysis for Social Scientists.* London: Routledge.

Pilcher, D.M. (1990) *Data Analysis for the Helping Professions: A Practical Guide.* London: Sage.

All the above books deal with the use of statistical methods in psychological and social science research and so describe techniques which may be applicable to research in counselling.

Box 6.4   Some counselling and psychotherapy journals

American Journal of Psychotherapy
Behavioural Psychotherapy
British Journal of Cognitive Psychotherapy
British Journal of Guidance and Counselling
British Journal of Psychotherapy
Changes
Counseling Psychologist
Counselling
Counselling Psychology Review
Counselling Psychology Quarterly
Gestalt Journal
International Journal for the Advancement of Counselling
International Journal of Eclectic Psychotherapy
International Journal of Group Psychotherapy
Journal of Counseling and Development
Journal of Counseling Psychology
Journal of Family Therapy
Journal of Integrative and Eclectic Psychotherapy
Journal of Rational Emotive Behaviour Therapy
Person Centred Practice
Person Centred Review
Psychotherapy
Psychotherapy Research
Self and Society
Transactional Analysis Journal

departments or universities publish a prospectus which includes an indication of the research interests of the academic staff. This can be a useful way of discovering who may be able and interested to offer supervision. The research literature too may provide a guide to suitable sources of supervision. A critical reading will indicate who or what institutions are working in similar or sympathetic areas to the proposed research.

Summary

Contributions to the furtherance of knowledge are essential to keep counselling and psychotherapy alive, vibrant and vital. This may be informal or structured and systematic. More formal processes include running a workshop, writing for publication and engaging in research.

Running a workshop is an ideal way for many practitioners to communicate their knowledge and skills. Workshops may be offered at conferences, as part of a course programme or promoted independently.

Writing for publication is a way in which practitioners may offer their knowledge and experience to the profession as a whole. Publications take many forms – these include letters to editors, book reviews, papers or articles or books.

A journal article is the most appropriate way of conveying ideas, experiences, discoveries or opinions at moderate length. There is space for contributions of many kinds. Outlets include academic, professional and specialist journals.

Practitioners wishing to publish an article are advised to consider their audience and an appropriate journal and to write accordingly. Submitting a paper to a journal does not guarantee its acceptance for publication. Papers are considered by the journal editor and submitted to referees for their opinion and advice. Feedback from these sources enables authors to refine their work.

Writing a book is a major undertaking and the advice of someone who has already written one may be helpful. Publishers are willing to consider formal and structured proposals for books.

Even though it has a reputation to the contrary, research is an ordinary activity. Research addresses not only effectiveness and outcome but also the experiences of clients and therapists. Quantitative methods have a place in counselling research but qualitative methods which deal with the subjective experiences clients and therapists have of therapy are of increasing importance.

The research process, the quest to answer a burning question, can be about the professional and personal development of the practitioner. Research is cyclical involving observation, reflection, experimentation and review.

Research may lead to a higher degree (MA/MSc, MPhil, PhD). Registration may be full or part time. Institutions offer supervision by an experienced researcher, training in research methods and access to library and computing facilities.

7

Resourcing Your Self

> One of the greatest lessons I have learned is that of taking care of myself: that includes physically, emotionally and spiritually. I have recognised an increasing need for time for myself: aerobics, reading for pleasure, meals with friends, etc. all of which I need to plan for in order to make them happen. (Liz Nicholls, counsellor, North West Centre for Eating Disorders, personal communication, 1995)

Personal and professional development is not solely about pushing back limitations, nor is it about meeting the requirements of the professional organisations: it is about preserving and maintaining what is good and it is about working in a way which is personally meaningful. Just as counsellors have an obligation to continually address their development, so they have an obligation to maintain themselves in a state 'fit to practise'. It is this need that Nicholls recognises and which she sees as essential to her ability to function as a counsellor. I agree with Nicholls that something which contributes to my abilities and safety as a practitioner is the attention I pay to myself and my own needs. By taking time to relax and to enjoy myself, by attending to my social relationships and my physical, emotional and spiritual needs outside the counselling relationship, I can ensure that I meet my clients in a refreshed state and without danger of meeting *my* needs in the therapeutic encounter or failing to offer my clients my full attention and all my skills and abilities. This I consider to be the obligation of anyone working as a therapist and to be a legitimate concern in the context of professional and personal development. In times of life crisis this is likely to be doubly important. Orlans (1993: 62–67) has written movingly of the effect of the break up of her marriage on her practice as a counsellor:

> Grieving is an exhausting process and I have frequently felt tired and in need of much support. Over time I have learnt to keep clearer

boundaries between work and leisure, I have on occasion cut down my work load considerably, I have called on the support of close friends and have made it a priority to maintain these important contacts, and have gained energy and support at different times from Chinese medicine, acupuncture, massage and cranial osteopathy. In the course of this, I have developed a wealth of useful tips for clients as well as proving to myself that only when I am prepared to take care of *me* can I authentically take care of others.

Orlans and Nicholls share the conviction that time for their own social and emotional relationships and the process of being attentive to themselves make them better counsellors. Orlans views her experience of dealing with the breakdown of her marriage as contributing 'significantly to my current and potential effectiveness as a counsellor'. She says that this is because of her 'constant wish' to learn from her experiences, which she acknowledges is sometimes a struggle. This reflects my experience. It is by accepting that at times my life is stressful and painful and making allowances for myself, not acting as if I was not susceptible to the same difficulties as my clients, that I have continued to grow as a person and as a professional. Recognising that I need not expect myself to be the 'perfect' counsellor has been a liberation. If I don't have to be perfect then it is easier to recognise and deal with my 'weaknesses' (which when acknowledged and faced often turn out to be strengthening) and my foibles.

Counsellors have some more or less 'institutional' strategies for coping with both extraordinary and mundane life events. Supervision is one way in which counsellors seek to ensure their effectiveness and that they are 'safe' to practise. Good use of supervision goes a long way to deal with some of the tensions that result from working with clients. Supervision is also a place in which the needs of the practitioner for 'rest and recuperation' may become apparent or can be discussed, but it isn't necessarily a way in which these needs may be satisfied. Personal therapy may also have a role to play in the maintenance of the health of the counsellor but it too is unlikely to offer everything a counsellor needs. Practising therapists may benefit from taking positive steps towards stress management and/or relaxation and are likely to benefit from managing their time in such a way as to allow for other activities, including constructive contact with people who are not their clients. Some programme of self-maintenance is therefore a valuable part of a strategy for professional and personal development.

The art of self-maintenance

In any sphere of life, people are exposed to stress and being a therapist is no exception. At least one complete book (Dryden, 1995) is devoted to the stresses of being a counsellor. Issues addressed include an 'integrative research review' of stress in counsellors, the stresses of working with specific client groups (e.g. clients who have been sexually abused and those with a disability), the stresses encountered in different counselling contexts (e.g. general practice) and the stresses encountered in counsellor education. The inference to be drawn from this is that counselling is (or can be) stressful to the counsellor. Such stress must be released, or at least managed.

Some client behaviours induce stress in counsellors. Brady et al. (1995: 2–5) discuss these; and find that the most stressful clients are those who are suicidal. They also consider aggressive and/or violent clients, depressed clients, clients who complain of unethical behaviour or malpractice, terminally ill clients and clients suffering from a personality disorder. They also report that working conditions may contribute significantly to counsellor stress. Organisational politics, excessive administrative tasks and high workloads are prime factors.

Too much stress reduces quality of life and increases the likelihood of disease and burnout. Brady et al. (1995: 8) cite evidence to suggest that emotional depletion is directly linked to burnout, and say that 'When the emotional drain from work-related factors is so great that it hinders personal and professional functioning, the therapist is likely to be suffering from burnout.' Lockley (1995: 265) describes the symptoms of burnout as an inability to escape a condition of emotional and physical exhaustion. He writes that counsellors

> can feel continually tired, lethargic, unable to sleep. They may suffer from physical ailments such as frequent headaches, backache, stomach complaints or other often rather vague symptoms. . . . There are also psychological signs such as disillusionment, self-doubt, doubts about the value of personal work and the work of the agency, feelings of helplessness and being trapped in one's job, a sense of not being appreciated and one's hard work being taken for granted.

Burnout can contribute to illness such as heart disease, ulcers and asthma and to emotional difficulties such as depression. Unless it is checked, or better still prevented, burnout may lead the counsellor to become neglectful or even abusive of clients. This switch from helper (perhaps through helplessness) to 'abuser' (either through action or through neglect) is analogous to the transactional analysis 'drama triangle' (see Stewart and Joines, 1987: 236–238).

For the therapist, taking steps to counter the effects of professional and personal stress becomes a professional obligation. Personal therapy is one way in which this might be achieved but there are others. Lockley (1995: 263–283) writes about 'the whole area of counselling stress and how best it can be managed'. Management includes strategies for the prevention of burnout and the alleviation of stress.

Because our responses to stress are highly individual, any programme for the management or prevention of stress should also be individual, matching the personality, needs and lifestyle of the person for whom it is intended. A symposium, 'Stress Management and Counselling' (Dryden and Palmer, 1994: 5–81) addressed a range of approaches and interventions. These included a rationale for a biological approach to stress management, a person centred approach, an account of rational emotive behaviour therapy in the treatment of stress, and papers addressing stress at work.

Stress management is basically about acquiring and implementing skills and strategies. The most helpful of these will vary from individual to individual but what is common is to find ways of changing the thinking, emotions, behaviour and lifestyle which lead to undue stress. Stress management is about learning to recognise and control pressures and demands from within and without as well as becoming proficient in controlling mental, emotional and behavioural responses to those demands. This leads to increased awareness, self-confidence and self-control, and hence personal growth.

Stress is contributed to by the unrealistic expectations counsellors sometimes have of themselves. Lockley (1995: 270) lists counsellor beliefs which may contribute to feelings of stress:

- Counsellors should not make mistakes.
- Counsellors should always arrive at the best solutions.
- Counsellors always have to know what they are doing.
- Counsellors are responsible for what happens to their clients.
- Counsellors should be successful in work with clients.

To these, I would add:

- Counsellors do not have personal problems.
- Counsellors should put their clients before themselves.

For me, these add up to a belief that the counsellor should be perfect. This isn't actually true. This spurious drive for perfection is damaging to the health of the counsellor and may not be of benefit to the client. Whether a counsellor believes in the importance of transference and counter-transference in the counselling relationship, the primacy of congruence or takes a skills approach to client work, an inability to allow for mistakes and human weaknesses on the part of the counsellor is unlikely to facilitate the client's growth or learning. Developing strategies for the prevention or management of stress (see Box 7.1) therefore becomes incumbent upon practitioners.

Rest and recreation

recreation: the act of creating anew: a new creation: refreshment after toil, sorrow etc.: pleasurable occupation of leisure time: an amusement or sport: a source of amusement. (*Chambers Twentieth Century Dictionary*)

Looking after yourself can be fun! Kottler (1986: 140) states that many practitioners choose adventure (actual or vicarious) as a form of therapy. Certainly 'escaping' into a book or film is a way of switching off from the trials and tribulations of therapeutic work. These may have the added advantage that, because they are about human interactions, they increase knowledge of humanity and human processes. One of my former students reported her initial puzzlement when she presented a difficulty with her client work to her supervisor. He recommended that she read a particular novel. She came to appreciate the wisdom of her supervisor's response. Not only did her reading entertain her (and give her time and space from which she benefited) but she found that her knowledge of people was considerably increased. Subsequently, she often found out more about herself and her clients from fiction than she did from counselling texts.

Real adventure too can offer respite and refreshment. Holidays 'away from it all' allow recuperation and an opportunity to regain perspective on what is important. Getting away from it all may

Box 7.1 Strategies for the prevention of stress

- *Exercise* – which not only promotes physical health but has a beneficial effect on the mind. So, take a stroll in the park at lunchtime, take the dog out, play football, join a step class, take up running or in some other way decline to join the increasing number of people defined as 'sedentary'.

- *Meditation* including any deliberate attempt to set aside time for quiet, contemplative activity. Meditation is associated with Eastern mystical and religious practices (and many local Buddhist groups offer classes) but it has a place in the Western tradition too. At its simplest, meditation is the process of focusing the mind on one stimulus to the exclusion of others. This stimulus can be a sound, a picture, internal body-rhythms (e.g. the breath) or even 'emptiness'. Meditation improves concentration and enhances alertness as well as reducing stress.

- *Healthy eating*: alcohol, caffeine, etc. contribute to raised levels of stress. It is probably true that 'a little of what you fancy does you good' but many foodstuffs affect the body and/or the mind. Dietary imbalance or over-indulgence is likely to be at least physically stressful. Some of this is known from folk knowledge (e.g. eating cheese late at night causes nightmares), some from scientific investigation (e.g. chocolate contains a powerful brain-active chemical and – more contentiously – some food colourings are associated with 'hyperactivity').

- *Adequate rest and sleep*: sleep deprivation can result in a state similar to drunkenness. Physical functioning is impaired and the absence of an opportunity to dream results in hallucinations.

- *Countering irrational beliefs* (rational emotive behaviour therapists take the view that people contribute to their own stress by habitually reinforcing their irrational beliefs). For example, Palmer (1995b: 148) considers the irrational belief 'I must be an outstanding therapist'. He writes that a counsellor 'can consider the three common disputes'. These are:

Logical: Although it is strongly preferable to be an outstanding therapist, how does it logically follow that I *must* be one? ANSWER: It does not logically follow.
Empirical: There is plenty of evidence that I strongly desire to be an outstanding therapist but where is the evidence that I *must* be an outstanding therapist? or, Where is it written that I *must* be an outstanding therapist? ANSWER: There is no evidence anywhere, nor is it written anywhere (apart from inside my own head) that I must be an outstanding therapist.
Pragmatic: If I carry on holding on to the belief that I *must* be an outstanding therapist, where is it going to get me? ANSWER: Whether my clients improve or

do not improve, either way I will remain anxious and paradoxically my anxiety will reduce my effectiveness. This is exactly what I don't want.

Palmer takes the view that once counsellors have disputed these 'unhelpful' beliefs a more helpful coping statement may be developed thus:

Coping statement: Although it is strongly preferable and desirable to be an outstanding therapist I don't have to be one. I'll just do my best whenever I can.

Feltham (personal communication, 1996) offers the thought that it may be equally irrational to believe 'I must continually strive to actualise myself, to become a fully functioning person, to develop personally and professionally' and implies that this belief could be treated in a similar way. Whatever the belief, a way of reducing stress is to re-examine personal 'musts', 'shoulds' and 'oughts' and to be more accepting and allowing of greater flexibility.

- *Relaxation, yoga etc.*: like meditation, whole body relaxation of the type taught in anxiety management classes has a calming and restful effect. Yoga, T'ai Chi and related 'exercise' systems address the complex of body, mind and spirit and offer ways of integrating these. Kingsland and Kingsland (1976: 14–15) describe Hatha yoga (which is the branch of yoga most widely practised in the West) as 'an integrated system of personal development by which the vicissitudes of life can be transcended, psychosomatic tensions can be removed and personal horizons can be extended'.
  Similar claims are made for T'ai Chi.

involve travel to an exotic location, a formal retreat or a fortnight in the garden, but even a walk in the country, a shopping trip or going to a concert or a sporting event may constitute a therapeutic break.

'Recreation' is about more than having fun. The dictionary definition above includes the concept of making anew or refreshing (i.e. making fresh once more). It is this renewal that is important to continuing development. Relaxing, resting and being entertained all contribute to the growth of a counsellor and a personal programme may profitably include the opportunity for them.

Creative approaches to relaxation

'Relaxation' has a colloquial usage close in meaning to some definitions of recreation. It can mean being more or less inactive or indulging in a pastime or pursuit unrelated to day-to-day tasks. In the context of health care, it has another meaning: that of inducing a state of reduced mental, emotional and physical tension. In this meaning, relaxation is a state of reduced activity of the sympathetic nervous system and a relaxation response is the opposite of a stress response. Deliberately inducing this state may be beneficial to practitioners.

The benefits of this form of relaxation (perhaps familiar from yoga, antenatal classes or anxiety management) are said to include increased physical well-being (perhaps because the release of muscular tension enables blood and hormones to circulate freely), decreased susceptibility to anxiety and to exhaustion, increased self-confidence and improved mental functioning. Trower et al. (1988: 121) consider this form of relaxation to be a skill acquired through the practice of a series of exercises. The most familiar are exercises in which groups of muscles throughout the body are systematically tensed and relaxed. Other techniques include those which emphasise controlled breathing and those based in creative visualisation. For example, Chaplin (1988: 94–95) writes about a breathing technique and 'some relaxation work that involved imaging warm energy rising from "mother earth" through [the client's] feet and legs and into the rest of her body'.

In Chaplin's example, the creative and imaginative facilities are being invoked as facilitators of a relaxed state. The whole body relaxation techniques taught in cognitive behavioural approaches to counselling and in yoga and meditation with which they are associated are very important ways of inducing a relaxed state – but they are not the only means. Relaxation can be fun and can make use of the creative and expressive energies of human beings in active and energetic ways. Parsons (1995: 25–26) writes about the 'laughter cure'. He reports anecdotal and research evidence to support the idea that 'laughter is the best medicine'. Kierr (1995: 129) writes of her use of dance and movement in the management of anxiety. Working with art materials, creative writing and music are all potential pathways to a relaxed state. Natalie Rogers (1985) describes and discusses what she calls 'the creative connection'. In her approach to expressive therapy, creative methods are used sequentially to facilitate growth, healing and understanding. For example, clay work might be followed by work with shape and colour, followed by movement, followed by creative writing. As the form of expression is changed, so the theme, feeling or sense becomes more apparent – this is the creative connection. Silverstone (1994: 18–23) would consider this to be a way of opening channels to the right hemisphere of the brain which she says is 'non-verbal, spatial, spontaneous, intuitive, creative and non-judgmental'. The integration of these qualities with those of the left brain (thinking, analysis, judgement, verbal skills), Silverstone writes, 'could bring about the ability to function more fully'.

In belief in the power of the creative connection and an awareness that movement and all forms of expression tend to reduce tension (and therefore induce a more relaxed state) and because I know of the links between fun and enjoyment and a sense of well-being, I have made extensive use of expressive approaches to therapy with clients who are anxious, tense or exhausted. For them and myself, this approach has been very effective and I think it could profitably be a part of any counsellor's programme of ensuring personal fitness. Working with art materials is a way of accessing and expressing feelings, creative writing is a channel to the mind and movement is a way of integrating mind, body and perhaps spirit. All of these activities are useful de-stressors but together they are more than the sum of their parts.

Reading for pleasure and professional development

> Wouldn't you welcome the opportunity to counsel Dorothea? Think of how much she endured, so painfully with Casaubon. Such cruelty inflicted on such a wonderful human being. (Catherine Foxon, counsellor, speaking of the characters in George Eliot's *Middlemarch*, personal communication, 1994)

Reading fiction can be a form of escapism. I regularly journey into the farthest reaches of time and space swept along by the 'what if' notions of science fiction writers. This undoubtedly provides me with amusement and helps me 'unwind' when the work of the day is over. This in itself is a good enough reason for reading but there are others. Reading may be a constructive way of contributing to professional and personal development. Annette Blampied, a counselling practitioner and counselling trainer, says that, in her view, counselling trainees can learn as much (or more) about human nature and ways of being with people from reading a novel as they can from any counselling text (personal communication, 1993). She adds that reading fiction is also likely to be more enjoyable!

What is true for the trainee is equally true for the practitioner. Knights (1995: 1) in a book about the relevance of imaginative literature to the practice of counselling writes about the importance of reading for counsellors. Arguing that an encounter with a text is of itself a valuable developmental interaction almost regardless of its content, Knights says:

> I propose that willingness to 'stay with' the encounter with texts actually contributes to the hinterland of personality in the individual reader, and so has a direct bearing upon their working self.

and continues:

> I am suggesting that, attentively read, novels, plays, or poems, develop our empathy, our imagination, our repertoire of names for situations. (ibid.: 6)

I would go further than that. My own reading has indeed offered me insight into how others might think, feel and act but it has also encouraged me to think about professional issues. There are other ways in which imaginative literature may contribute to professional development. In the quotation above, Foxon is describing a counselling equivalent of the 'thought experiments' of physics. She used her imagination to understand fictional characters and how they might respond to her professional skills. To do this, she thought about each of them in terms of the approach to counselling she adopts (she went on to talk about Dorothea's 'inadequate self-concept' and her ability to become 'fully functioning'). Whether the conclusions Foxon reached are 'right' is not relevant: that she used her imaginative and creative abilities to further her understanding is.

In the analytic tradition, there are examples of the analysis of fictional characters and analytic interpretations of myth and fairy tale (see Bettelheim, 1976). Examined from this viewpoint, 'Little Red Riding Hood' is understood as a tale of menarche, 'Cinderella' as a warning about incest and abuse and I suppose that the beanstalk in 'Jack and the Beanstalk' is a rather obvious phallic symbol!

Any reading of fiction and poetry *may* contribute to personal and professional development (and, arguably it all does) but some

---

Box 7.2   Fiction likely to be of use to counsellors (a selection from Ben Knights *The Listening Reader,* **1995)**

- Abuse of children and young people – *The Color Purple,* Alice Walker; *The Man Who Loved Children,* Christina Stead; *The Wasp Factory,* Iain Banks

- Alcoholism – *Under the Volcano,* Malcolm Lowry

- Death – *The Death of Ivan Illych,* Tolstoy; 'I heard a fly buzz when I died' ('Dying'), Emily Dickinson

- Gender – *The Summer before the Dark,* Doris Lessing; *Praxis,* Fay Weldon; *Woman on the Edge of Time,* Marge Piercy

- Madness – *Pasmore,* David Storey; *Beyond the Glass,* Antonia White; *King Lear,* Shakespeare

- Unemployment – *Love on the Dole,* Walter Greenwood

---

texts may be particularly appropriate for counsellors. Knights (1995: 115–126) offers a list of these and arranges them by topic (see Box 7.2 for some examples).

Knights also gives a guide to authors and a booklist which focuses on the uses of literature to therapy.

Knights does not claim to have produced the definitive reading list for counsellors. Many people will have other title(s) to recommend, some book, poem, play or story from which they have derived support, ideas or understanding. Perhaps the best advice with respect to reading for pleasure *and* development is to read what you enjoy, test out the recommendations of people you know and respect, and experiment (at least occasionally). Whether you read the classics of English literature such as the works of Austen or the Brontës, become absorbed in the novels of Dostoevsky, the intricacies of Umberto Eco, tales of black experience from Alice Walker, Toni Morrison or the poems of Derek Walcott, or indulge in fantasy and escapism, reading can be a passport to an increased understanding of human nature and interactions.

Keeping a personal journal and the use of creative writing

From reading the writing of others, it is (conceptually at least) but a small step to writing yourself. I am not necessarily suggesting that counsellors should write novels and/or poetry (although each might have a role in development!) but that a record of thoughts, feelings and encounters has a function in professional and personal development.

The keeping of a personal journal in which the practitioner's emotional and cognitive processes, details of reactions to inter-actions with friends, colleagues and clients, and (perhaps) dreams are recorded may provide a rich source upon which to reflect. This reflection may result in deeper understanding of both the therapist's self and others and perhaps lead to new ideas. Jung kept a diary which he called his Black Book in which, as Kottler (1986: 135) states, 'He first developed his theories; analysed his dreams, fantasies, and symbols; recorded the events of his life; and conducted imaginary dialogues with his unconscious.' Kottler writes that: 'In the role of confidant to others, a structure must be created for the therapist to become a confidant to himself' (ibid.: 136). In his opinion, systematic journal writing does just that in the following ways:

It is a way to supervise oneself and work through difficulties with particular cases.
It is a method of self-analysis.
It is a vehicle for developing and recording ideas.
It is a record of significant events.

For these reasons, journal keeping offers not only a type of self-therapy but a way of monitoring development and a basis from which to determine developmental needs. It can also provide a form of catharsis, as might writing letters to friends and col-leagues. Sometimes writing as if to a client (with no intention of actually sending or delivering the letter) may be a helpful way of dealing with the practitioner's personal reactions – indeed writing any letter doesn't mean that it must be read by the addressee. This opens the possibility of writing to anyone: living, dead, yet to be, real or imagined. I use this technique in the 'creative approaches to supervision' groups that I facilitate and counsellors report that it is useful both to their understanding of the client/counsellor relationship and to their development.

The usefulness of creative writing in professional development is not confined to the writing of letters. The 'what if?' nature of creative writing allows for the intuitive exploration of many situations. In the context of creative approaches to supervision, I invite supervisees to imagine that they are marooned on a desert island with a client. My invitation is to write the story of 'what happens next?' The use of creative writing is not confined to supervision.

Less structured and more spontaneous writing may also be a valid form of personal development. Bolton (1995) in a paper about therapeutic writing discusses the advantages of this to the therapist as well as writing as a way of working with clients. The processes she describes are more to do with creativity and the expression of the intuitive part of a person and she has no doubt of the value of this to herself and to other therapists.

Dreams and dreaming

Working with dreams has a long tradition in the practice of psychotherapy. This is true not only of the analytic tradition but of the humanistic tradition (for example in Gestalt and psychodrama) and in transpersonal approaches (such as psychosynthesis). Just as this may be an effective and valuable way of working with clients so it may be a way for practitioners to tune into their creative and imaginative selves – this may be a path to professional and personal development. Rowan (1983: 94) describes three broad ways of working with dreams. These involve seeing dreams as:

- to do with the past. This is the traditional psychoanalytic approach in which the dream is retrospective and provides Freud's 'Royal road to the unconscious'.
- about the present. This is the approach taken in Gestalt and existential approaches and in which the dream or its elements may be understood as projections of the 'here and now'.
- about the future. This is the Jungian approach where dreams represent aspirations and directions in life.

Rowan emphasises that dreams, because they are symbolic, may work on all these levels and Jacobs (1988: 7) writes that 'modern psychodynamic theory understands the different figures in dreams as representing various aspects of the self' which sounds similar to a Gestalt understanding. Gendlin (1986) writes about letting 'your body interpret your dreams'. He offers sixteen questions to aid interpretation, which he sees as having two stages. Gendlin's first stage is identifying what the dream is about and his second is getting something new from the dream. The latter is difficult because we each tend to interpret our own dreams in terms of our particular bias. Gendlin writes about 'bias control' as a way of circumventing this and thus bestowing an ability to interpret dreams in a new, meaningful and useful way.

Mahrer (1971: 328) states that 'an individual can bring about change in himself or in others by the systematic use of dreams'. He proposes seven steps (see Box 7.3) 'as one way of enabling oneself to undergo personality-behaviour change' and illustrates these with reference to a particular dream.

Dreams may serve not only as a pathway to personality and/or behavioural change but also as a state of consciousness in which 'problem-solving' may occur. Dean Juniper, a counselling tutor (personal communication, 1984), spoke of the value of paying attention to dreams and to hypnagogic and hypnopompic experiences (that is experiences in the stages between waking and sleeping and sleeping and waking respectively) especially when tackling a seemingly intractable problem. The chemist Kekule is reputed to have solved the problem of the structure of the benzene molecule while dozing. He and his colleagues had been struggling with the problem for some time until one day, in his sleep, Kekule saw six snakes dancing with each other. Eventually each of these snakes seized the tail of another in its jaws: the resulting six-sided figure is said to have led Kekule to the recognition of the ring structure of the benzene molecule.

Whatever use dreams are to be put to, they are only useful inasmuch as they are remembered or recalled. Dream workers seem to be unanimous in their belief that immediate recording is most facilitative to the exploration and use of dreams and many advocate keeping a dream diary. It seems too that a deliberate effort to recall dreams brings an increasing ability to do so and makes your dreams more vivid, complete and relevant to waking life. If you wish to recall and work with your dreams, the suggestions in Box 7.4 may be useful.

The creative and caring self as an agent of development

The creation of stories and poems, the use of myth and fairy tale – said by Dufeu (1994: 129) to 'represent a means of contact with

Box 7.3   Seven steps to life change through dreaming (after Mahrer, 1971: 328–332)

1. *Selecting the dream.* Immediately recalled dreams are more useful than old ones, emotionally charged dreams are more useful than those low in feeling, vivid dreams are more useful than those lacking in detail.

2. *Recording the dream.* Record the dream as soon as possible either on audio tape or in writing. Make this recording complete in terms of each feeling (and its intensity) and all detail. Each action, object, person and surrounding should be reported 'graphically'.

3. *Linking the dream to recent events.* Identify the links between the dream and your current life – this should be done as soon as possible after recording. To establish these links ask the following questions about each element of the dream.

   - During the last few days, what were the exact circumstances in which I saw, thought about, fantasised, imagined or attended to that particular element?
   - What was going on in me (in my feelings and behaviours) during those exact circumstances?

4. *Identifying the motivation.* The fourth step is to identify the drive, behavioural tendency, potential way of being, wish, need or goal toward which you are striving. The presumption is that the motivation comes closest to expression during the moment when the peak of feeling occurs in the dream.

5. *Identifying the critical recent life event.* Frame a fuller and more psychologically meaningful description of the critical recent life event on the basis of what you have gained from the dream.

6. *Experiencing the motivation.* Experience the motivation within the context of that dream-revised recent life event. Give up control over the motivation. This means giving up your typical way of being and letting the motivation take you over completely, experiencing it fully. *Be* the motivation – surrender to it and experience a complete release. This occurs when you have the naked feelings of total experiencing. The horror and terror *about* the motivation are replaced by a new aliveness. Allow internal integration – hold the experience at its peak and let it happen. Personality change occurs in the very act of holding the peak moment of experiential actualisation.

7. *Facilitating new behaviours.* Your peak dream feelings are your reactions to your potential ways of behaving. If they are negative then your relationship with the deeper motivation is disintegrated and you are not yet ready for behavioural change. Positive peak feelings indicate a readiness for transformation.

Box 7.4   Recording dreams (after Garfield, 1976)

1. Remind yourself before sleeping that you will remember your dreams.
2. When you know you have just dreamt, lie still and with closed eyes, let images flow into your mind.
3. When you feel that your dream recall is complete in the position in which you awoke, slowly and gently move into other sleeping positions that you use (eyes still closed). You will find that you recall additional material.
4. Record your dreams in the order that you recall them. Garfield says that this should preferably be with eyes still closed – an audio tape might be useful.
5. Record a unique verbal expression immediately, noting your unique productions first and trying to identify the elusive elements of your dream.
6. If possible, share your dreams with a friend as well as recording them.
7. Select titles for your dreams from their unique characteristics.

---

the deepest sources of our imagination' – and the reading of the works of others may all have a part to play in both professional and personal development. According to taste, the same is true of dance and movement, work with colour and shape, voice and music, drama and fantasy. However they are utilised, the creative and imaginative energies common to human beings have the power to assist in transformation and growth. Just as this is true of personal development or therapy (what helps a client change also helps a counsellor change!) it is true of professional development.

To enter the realm of the imagination, to tune into and make use of the creative force, is to contact a speculative 'what if?' dimension and 'worlds within oneself, which have a character of otherness' (Dufeu, 1994: 21). This can aid an understanding of the experiences of others and increases the acceptance of the strange and unfamiliar. Dufeu writes:

> Through creative activities we learn to establish new relationships between things, and to perceive different aspects of reality; this can lead to a broadening or restructuring of our perception of reality.
>
> This change in perception, this fresh perspective, often provides a basis for change and helps bring about a different attitude to our reality. Instead of accepting things as they are, we start to act upon them and to develop innovative attitudes.

I agree with Dufeu that creative activities can lead to an increased awareness and enhanced perception and the broadening of imaginative facilities is invaluable to counsellors and therapists of all kinds. I believe it to be important that continuing development comprises more than academic learning and the acquisition of skills. It should also be a creative process with elements of spontaneity and fun.

Besides works addressing the way in which creative energies can be used by practitioners to enhance their personal and professional development, there are a number of 'self-help' books which may be useful. The 'Popular Psychology' shelves of bookshops tend to be heavy with such works, ranging from those with a behavioural bias to those which are decidedly mystical in their philosophy. It really is a case of paying your penny and taking your choice. Some such books have a more clearly 'counselling' bias. For example, Rowan (1993) has written about how you might identify your sub-personalities, Ferrucci (1982) offers psychosynthesis exercises which facilitate personal integration and spiritual development, Gendlin (1986) writes about dream interpretation from a 'focusing' viewpoint, Ernst and Goodison (1981) have produced a practical guide to self-help therapy using techniques drawn from many approaches, McCormick (1996) has written an 'easily followed programme to develop insights into old patterns' based on cognitive analytic therapy and Burns's (1989) 'self-help' book is rooted in the techniques of cognitive therapy.

Just as the development of counsellors may be facilitated by creation and 'artistic' expression, so it will be by the exercise of care and attention towards their self (body, mind and spirit). Counsellors have a 'duty of care' towards their clients but also towards themselves. No programme of development is complete without an element which addresses rest, relaxation, recuperation and recreation. It is incumbent upon practitioners to find ways of repaying themselves with kindness. The advertisers of Mars Bars recognised the benefits of an holistic approach long ago. Counsellors should include not only 'work' in their programmes but also 'rest and play'!

Although I consider self-help, the development of creative and imaginative energies, adequate rest and relaxation essential to professional development (and to good practice) it is unlikely that an accrediting organisation would recognise these as sufficient continuing development. It is only as part of an holistic package that they will be valued.

Keeping up to date

Changes in the profession of counselling and psychotherapy tend to occur frequently. Some of these changes are seemingly relatively minor (perhaps a change in a code of ethics), some (like a whole new approach) seem more important. Emphasis on cost-effectiveness (and perhaps ethical considerations) have led to an interest in short interventions and the birth of brief therapy: cognitive analytic therapy has sprung partly from this desire for short but effective therapy and partly from the recognition of things of value in both the traditions which inform it. As important as these developments are, individual practitioners might be more directly affected by changes in the code of ethics and practice of the organisation to which they belong. For instance, in 1992 the BAC *Code of Ethics and Practice for Counsellors* was amended in such a way as to state that it was unethical for counsellors to engage in sexual activity with their ex-clients until at least twelve weeks after the therapeutic relationship had ended. Lots of practitioners had strong and emotional reactions to this amendment. It was hotly debated at the conference and spawned letters to *Counselling* and at least one article (Wilkins, 1994).

As well as changes in the theory and practice of counselling there are changes in the 'politics' of the profession. There are debates about training (should it be academic, lead to a degree or diploma from a university, should it be practical and based in the NVQ system?), debates about registers of practitioners (should registration be mandatory, who is eligible for registration, which of the professional organisations is most credible in the eyes of government?). Updating, keeping abreast of these changes, innovations and developments, is a legitimate part of continuing development.

How might a practitioner be aware of and pursue information about important developments and current debates in counselling and psychotherapy? Conferences and the counselling press provide the easiest access to this material. The annual BAC training conference often has as its focus one of these 'hot' topics (for example 'Europeanisation' in 1991, counselling and psychotherapy in 1992); keynote speakers and plenary sessions will address it directly and workshops might too. Not all practitioners have the resources to enable them to attend conferences and so must depend upon the counselling press and their colleagues for this information. *Counselling* often publishes the keynote speeches from the annual conferences and its editorials, letters pages and articles often contain items of interest to practitioners interested in the current state of the art or the political debate. Most of the journals of the professional organisations have similar contents, as do publications like *Counselling News* and (to some extent) the academic journals. In addition, *Counselling* is occasionally produced as a 'special issue' in which many of the papers address a particular topic – in 1991 there was an issue on justice, in 1992 accreditation was a major topic and in 1994 it was the relevance of research to practice. Other journals (for instance the *British Journal of Guidance and Counselling*) also produce dedicated issues. Local groups may also arrange meetings to debate or consider issues of moment.

Resourcing yourself through resourcing others

Continuing development isn't merely about receiving; it can be about doing and giving. In the context of client work, being a trainer or supervisor, this may be obvious but there are other ways of contributing to the profession (and therefore your own development) through action. All the professional organisations for therapists, whether they have paid staff or not, depend upon members to sit on committees, organise and run sub-sections, referee papers and carry out peer assessment. The chairs or membership of these committees are often interested in hearing from suitably experienced people with the time and energy to contribute to their work. Similarly, journal editors may wish to hear from people who think that they can contribute as referees (relevant experience and some ability as a writer are necessary). The BAC process of accreditation and the UKCP process of registration depend upon peer review (in the latter this is organised by and within the constituent organisations) and again organising committees may be very pleased to hear from people who are themselves accredited/registered and who wish to be involved in the process.

Involvement in any of the above ways is likely to be viewed positively by assessors for accreditation, registration or chartering.

Although it can be costly in terms of time, generally it involves the practitioner in little or no expense and it might even be that expenses are offered. For some of these functions (for example becoming a member of an assessment team for accreditation) training is offered and this too contributes to the process of development. Lastly, committee service and active membership of a specialist section (for example counselling in medical settings section or RACE within the BAC) is an excellent way of keeping up with and even shaping the development of the profession.

Summary

Professional and personal development is about more than meeting the requirements of professional organisations. It is about preserving what is good and maintaining fitness to practise. This includes rest and relaxation as well as efforts to deepen or increase knowledge and to improve practice.

The practice of counselling and psychotherapy involves exposure to stress. This may arise from client behaviour, working conditions and the personal experiences of the practitioner. Countering the effects of stress (and therefore avoiding burnout) is a professional obligation. Personal therapy and supervision contribute to the prevention and alleviation of stress, as does stress management. Strategies for the prevention of stress include exercise, meditation, healthy eating, adequate rest, the countering of irrational beliefs, and relaxation techniques.

Having fun can also contribute to professional and personal development. Holidays, adventures and the like allow recuperation and an opportunity to regain perspective on what is important.

Deliberately inducing a relaxed state may be useful to practitioners. Yoga, breathing exercises and creative visualisation are some of the ways in which this may be done. Techniques from creative approaches to therapy are also useful.

Reading poetry and fiction may also contribute to development. As much (or more) can be learned about the human condition from reading a novel as from a psychology text (and the former also provides entertainment).

Writing in the form of a personal journal or of a creative nature is helpful to development. A journal in which the thoughts, feelings and experiences of the writer are recorded has a function in personal and professional development. Such a journal not only has a therapeutic function but may also provide a way of monitoring the progress of developmental strategies.

Dreams may provide a rich source of material to contribute to the process of development. This material is susceptible to psychodynamic interpretation *and* being worked with in humanistic and cognitive behavioural ways. Keeping a dream journal may be very helpful.

Creative and imaginative energies have the potential to facilitate transformation and growth. Using these faculties is a way of gaining insight into the experience of others and an enhanced awareness and perception.

Updating is a part of professional development. This is most easily achieved by, for example, attendance at conferences and local meetings and by continual reference to the letters, editorials and articles in the counselling and psychotherapy press.

Service to the profession in the form of, for example, committee membership is a legitimate form of professional development. This is also a way of keeping abreast of and shaping the development of the profession.

8

Determining a Personal Programme for Personal and Professional Development

An appropriate programme of continuing development will vary between individuals and will change with time. An effective programme should be designed in such a way as to meet the immediate needs of the individual counsellor and to lead towards any longer-term career ambitions. Such a programme should be constructed thoughtfully and evaluated (and if necessary adapted) regularly. A programme with evident purpose, achievable goals and a logical flow is not only much more likely to demonstrate a commitment to continuing development than an unformed, haphazard pattern of attendance at short courses or workshops but to be more satisfying to the counsellor. The very act of reflecting upon one's current state and status as a professional and any desired change can be stimulating and helpful. In this chapter I offer some ideas and suggestions as to how any counsellor might design, implement and review a personal programme of continuing development. The summary of what constitutes personal and professional development in Box 8.1 may be helpful in this task.

Box 8.1   Summary of kinds and methods of personal and professional development

Although professional and personal items appear in this box as separate entities, the reader should always bear in mind that in many ways the two are inseparable: each may contain elements of the other and what is professional development to one person may be personal development to another (and vice versa).

The suggestions as to the relative cost of the various types of development are intended only as a guide. More expensive instances may be found and the resourceful practitioner will undoubtedly be able to find effective development more cheaply.

PROFESSIONAL DEVELOPMENT

FURTHER TRAINING

Changing orientation: May involve another complete course but possibly facilitated by reading, working with a supervisor with the required expertise. A new course is likely to be *high cost*; a self-directed approach *low* or *no cost*.

Addressing gaps in training: All training courses are good at equipping their graduates for some things, less good at others. Gaps in awareness and expertise (widespread and of particular concern are those to do with cross-cultural issues and the law) may be addressed through reading, short courses and workshops. Addressing gaps is likely to be *medium* to *low cost*.

Higher qualification: Many universities and colleges offer higher degrees in counselling, psychotherapy or related topics. Master's degrees may be taught or by research, a PhD is normally offered as a research degree but some taught or part-taught programmes may be available. Study for a higher degree is likely to be *high* or *medium cost*.

Innovative approaches/expansion of skills: There are many approaches to therapy, many ideas about work in particular settings or with specific client groups. Practitioners wishing to acquire this knowledge or these skills may do so in a variety of ways but attendance at workshops or short courses may be especially effective. This activity is likely to be *medium* to *no cost*.

Reading: The literature of counselling and psychotherapy, both journals and books, increases at a rapid rate. Purposeful reading of, for example, classic texts, new approaches, etc. is (if use is made of libraries) a *low–no cost* form of development.

Keeping up to date: Professional updating on issues of ethics, theory and practice and the politics of counselling and psychotherapy is highly desirable. This is most easily achieved by attending the conferences of the professional organisations and other meetings of therapists, reading the counselling press and contributing to the development of the profession through (for example) committee work. Keeping up to date is *medium–no cost.*

PROFESSIONAL RECOGNITION
Accreditation (for members of the BAC), registration (for members of a constituent organisation of the UKCP) and chartering (for members of the counselling psychology section of the BPS) are possible roots to professional recognition. These involve practitioners in demonstrating that they are trained and competent representatives of the organisations to which they are applying. These processes may initially be *medium–low cost* and/or there may be an annual fee.

SUPERVISION
Supervision as development: Many of the functions of supervision relate to professional development, and the developmental needs of the supervisee change with growing confidence and expertise. Individual, group and peer supervision all have strengths with respect to professional development. Because it is obligatory in any case, development through supervision is available at *little or no extra cost.*

Supervision to clarify a programme of development: Supervision is a place in which it is legitimate for the practitioner to consider developmental needs and how these might be addressed. The supervisor's function is to facilitate this exploration. Because extra sessions may be required, this strategy is *low–no cost.*

Developing as a supervisor: Becoming a supervisor is a natural career progression for some therapists. There is an increasing number of training courses in supervision and practitioners seeking professional recognition as supervisors would be well advised to undertake such training. Training as a supervisor is *high–medium cost.*

CONTRIBUTING TO THE FURTHERANCE OF KNOWLEDGE
Disseminating skills: Offering practical expertise in the form of a workshop or short course is a pragmatic form of development. This is likely to involve *low–no cost* and might even be *rewarded.*
Writing for publication: Editors of journals constantly seek well-written papers relevant to the interests of their readers. Writing a paper (or a solicited book review) is a *no cost* form of development; writing a book (normally only undertaken by pre-arrangement with a publisher) is likely to generate *income.*
Conducting research: Research in the field of counselling and psychotherapy is aimed at developing the understanding of the process experienced by clients and therapists and perhaps contributing to the construction of theory and the development of practice. Research studies may be large in scope or confined to a particular experience or

incident and may be quantitative or qualitative. All practitioners are researchers at least to the extent that they endeavour to understand the experience of their clients. Research can be costly but can equally involve *low–no cost.*

PERSONAL DEVELOPMENT

PERSONAL THERAPY
Individual therapy: For many approaches to counselling (particularly psychodynamic and humanistic ones), individual therapy is viewed as highly desirable if not essential to the development of the practitioner. Individual therapy is often *high–medium cost.*

Group therapy: Group approaches to therapy do not offer the same degree of intimacy and confidentiality as individual therapy but they have other advantages. Group members can learn from and feed back to each other and there is much to be gained from interactions between them. Because the costs of the therapist's time is defrayed over more people, group therapy is *medium–low cost.*

RESOURCING YOUR SELF
Stress management: The professional life of a therapist is often stressful and too much stress reduces the quality of life and may contribute to disease and burnout. Deliberate attempts to relieve and/or manage stress are therefore desirable. Many strategies for stress management involve *no cost.*

Rest and recreation: Personal development can legitimately involve fun and adventure and certainly should involve deliberate efforts at rest. 'Holidays' are as *cheap* or *expensive* as you care to make them.

Creative approaches to relaxation: Relaxation can mean the deliberate inducement of a state of reduced mental, emotional and physical tension. As well as the well-known relaxation techniques of (for example) antenatal classes and yoga, this state (or something like it) can be achieved through creative processes. Creative approaches to relaxation may be *low–no cost.*

Reading for pleasure: Fiction and poetry offer ways of learning more about the human condition as well as being 'therapeutic' to the reader. It is the interaction with the text that provides the opportunity for development. Reading is a *low–no cost* activity.

Journal keeping and creative writing: Journals of experiences with clients and day-to-day activities and interactions provide a rich source for reflection and from this reflection there is the potential for growth. Similarly, the 'what if?' nature of creative writing allows for the intuitive exploration of many situations. Writing is a *no cost* activity.

Using your dreams: Dreaming is an activity which has long been held to be of value in development and not only in the analytic tradition. Recording and interpreting dreams is *cost-free.*

Resources

Any programme of professional and personal development is limited by the resources available to it. In this context, resources are likely to be principally those of money, time and other restrictions to access. Many opportunities for development (such as a further qualification or attendance at an international conference) are costly and perhaps beyond the means of many counsellors. Many other opportunities are not so expensive (e.g. research based on practice or a programme of reading – see Appendix, p. 165) and, if they are approached creatively, may offer development of at least equal validity. Sometimes (as for those seeking accreditation or recognition) an element of expenditure cannot be avoided and so must be budgeted.

Continuing development takes time (which, particularly for counsellors who are self-employed, may mean loss of income). Time spent on development is lost to client work, to friends and family and to the hundred and one other things we each find we need to do! Time is important in another respect. By its nature, continuing professional and personal development is progressive. A practical programme will have duration – time is a resource to be allocated and spent as wisely and purposefully as money!

Lastly, for some developmental opportunities there are other problems of access. It might be that the most obvious route to a counsellor's desired objective is in some way blocked. The course that would meet a counsellor's needs may be held too far away, the material needed for a research project may be unavailable, there may not be supervisees for a would-be trainee supervisor and so on. In these cases counsellors may think in terms of staged responses (can the same goal be achieved in steps which *are* accessible?) or alternatives. Sometimes there may be alternative routes to the same goal (perhaps a training need could be addressed through distance learning and/or intensive periods of attendance); sometimes it may be necessary to substitute a more practical goal.

With respect to resources, the initial questions for a counsellor planning a programme of self-development to ask are:

- What resources do I have available to meet this commitment?
- What will these resources allow me?
- Is this (or can I find a way of making it) sufficient?

If the answer to the third is 'No' then some serious restructuring may be necessary.

Just like supervision, continuing development is necessary for a practising counsellor. It is necessary because the codes of ethics and practice of the professional organisations demand it but more importantly because it is a way of ensuring a safe, competent service to clients. The commitment to continuing development has to be taken as seriously as the commitment to supervision. Most counsellors, recognising the necessity of supervision for their well-being and that of their clients, do not begrudge the costs. Similarly, employers of counsellors seem to be increasingly sympathetic to the professional need of counsellors for regular supervision. They are more willing to make time and money available for this.

Just as counsellors and other therapists have successfully made the case for supervision, convincing ourselves and those for whom we work of our need, so we must for continuing development. Counsellors in private practice may need to include an element for development in their costing of fees, those who work for agencies and institutions may need to make the argument with their managers. 'I can't afford it' is an unacceptable argument for the lack of supervision, and we should develop a similar attitude to continuing development (particularly because with respect to the latter there are low- or no-cost options). It is a commitment which accreditation and registration necessitate and perhaps one which increasingly pervades the culture of the profession as a whole. However, just as the quality of supervision is not necessarily related to how much it costs so it is with professional and personal development. A *relevant* personal programme of development should take account of both the needs and the means of the counsellor to whom it applies. The programme suitable (or achievable) for an unpaid counsellor working in a voluntary agency could be very different from the programme of a counsellor working full time for an institution, and counsellors from and/or working with minority groups may also have different needs and resources. The quality and *personal and professional relevance* of a programme of development are much more important than the time and money devoted to it.

Having decided the broad area of interest to be addressed through a continuing programme of development, the following questions may be worth asking:

1. What resources are available to me?
     How much money can I afford?
     How much time do I have?
     Can I gain access to the things I need?
2. Are these resources sufficient for my needs and/or my desires and to meet the requirements of my professional organisation?
3. If not, what can I do about it?
     Increase my resources?
     Moderate my needs and desires?
     Change my professional organisation?

Assessing developmental needs

Developmental needs include those arising from a counsellor's external circumstances and those which are more personal, arising from ambition and interest. The first may arise from a change of circumstances or responsibilities (like the example of 'Jane' encountering a new client group in Chapter 1) or from feedback from a supervisor or peers and may have a degree of urgency. The second (perhaps less urgent but certainly no less important) may relate to professional curiosity (e.g. a desire to learn about another approach to working with clients or to answer a 'research question') or career plans such as preparation for accreditation. To a certain extent, an effective programme of continuing development will also include an element in which forecasted needs are met. In this way, the need for the 'reactive' response to urgent need may be pre-empted.

A useful way of addressing the more urgent, 'reactive' issues may be to ask what is needed *now* to perform the immediate task? The second group of developmental needs may be determined by considering what is needed to enable any change in professional circumstances or what the counsellor must do to satisfy any ambition to work in another or additional way or to satisfy curiosity.

Questions to ask when planning a programme of development

Immediate or current needs
Each practitioner has an awareness of the current needs of their clients, agency or service and the extent to which they are able to meet them. This will involve counsellors reflecting upon their

professional ability and their personal resources in relation to the expectations they have of themselves and the requirements of clients and colleagues. Any shortfall indicates the first developmental issues to address in a well-constructed programme. To facilitate this, the very first questions to ask are 'diagnostic' (see Box 8.2).

The answers to these questions may provide useful indicators of desirable developmental strategies. Discussion with a supervisor and/or peers and colleagues may help determine which are the most appropriate and which have priority. A consideration of resources will indicate which of these needs may be practically met.

Longer-term developmental needs

Many counsellors have a clear idea about their medium- to long-term professional aims. Perhaps they are working towards accreditation or wish to become supervisors, perhaps they wish to write about their knowledge and experience or to conduct research, perhaps they are looking forward to retirement, perhaps they hope to contribute in some active way to the administering and policy-making of a professional organisation. For others, ambitions are less well defined. It may be that they see themselves as contented practitioners and have no desire to enter the scramble for professional advancement; their developmental needs are less those which offer a chance for change and more to do with maintaining a good and improving standard of service to their clients.

Perhaps it is important to realise that there may be an obsessive quality to the pursuit of professional development and that this may be counterproductive. For some counsellors, the anxiety about a particular group of clients leads them to continually seek 'training' which may actually interfere with 'doing'; for others the perpetual quest for yet another course can begin to appear neurotic – even personal therapy may acquire overtones of self-indulgence. Balance is important in continuing development: the amount of time devoted to it should be a reflection of a counsellor's experience and the amount of their practice.

Whatever stance an individual counsellor may take towards career development, there are some questions which are worth asking. Broadly speaking these are of the type given in Box 8.3.

All these question and others pertain to continuing development. Even in the (unlikely) event that the desire is for no change

---

Box 8.2   Questions pertaining to current needs

1. Is my current knowledge and ability and are my personal resources adequate to the needs and demands of my clients, colleagues and/or employers?

    This question may be addressed through reflection on work with clients, in supervision or in discussion with peers. Useful things to consider may be:

    - Are contracts terminating prematurely? This could indicate that clients are finding the counsellor unequal to the task.
    - Do clients seem reluctant or unable to address their personal material or to move on?
    - Are there issues, problems and difficulties that my clients bring that leave me feeling at a loss, inadequate, de-skilled or in some way troubled?
    - Are there some client issues that other counsellors commonly meet that I seldom or never meet?
    - Do I understand the culture, language and mores of my clients?
    - Am I feeling tired, jaded, depressed or resentful with respect to my work with clients?

2. If there seem to be undesirable limitations to my functioning as a counsellor are my needs professional (e.g. for more knowledge or enhanced skills) or personal (e.g. for personal therapy or rest and relaxation)?

    This question too may be answered through reflecting on a number of subsidiary questions such as:

    - Am I encountering clients of whom (or of whose issues) I know little? If so, could this be addressed through the acquisition of specialist knowledge? Are there short courses, workshops or books which would help me address any shortfall?
    - Are my skills and level of functioning as a counsellor adequate to the 'depth' and nature of the material my clients are presenting? If not, do I wish to enable myself to work in such a way? If so, would this be best addressed through an increased awareness of theory and practice or need I address my own material in therapy (or in some other way)?
    - Does the intensity of some clients scare me or leave me numb? Are there issues which my clients *never* bring to therapy? Are there emotions or issues to which I am 'deaf' (e.g. death and dying, anger, abuse, sexual issues, religious or spiritual issues), somehow failing to pick up on them? Do I consciously prefer not to deal with some issues? If so, is this because I perceive myself to be ignorant of them or because they remain unresolved for me?

- Does my work as a counsellor leave me drained and exhausted with little enthusiasm and energy for other things? Do I sometimes feel resentful of my clients, even angry and bitter towards them? Am I constantly aware of feelings of pressure, thinking of clients and their issues at weekends and in the evenings? If so, how can I relieve this pressure, become more alive and enthusiastic? Do I need to vary my work, perhaps developing other skills (e.g. supervision, training, writing) or would my interests and those of my clients and my colleagues be best served if I took deliberate steps to rest and to relax or to reduce my workload?

Box 8.3 Questions about longer-term developmental needs

What in (one year, five years, ten years, etc.) would I like to be different about:

- me, my knowledge and skills, my qualifications, my professional status, my self-awareness;
- my clients, the nature of their issues, their understanding, their age, their class;
- how I work, the techniques or approaches I use, the variety of my work;
- where I work, in what setting and for whom;
- how much I earn;
- for how many hours a week I work (with clients or at all).

---

in any of these elements, there are developmental issues of a kind. If this is so, then the principal issue is how to maintain a 'freshness' in the approach to clients. The developmental programme would centre on counsellors' needs to resource their selves in such a way as to be able to continue delivering a high quality, safe service.

The exact nature of the desired goal will determine the nature of the most appropriate developmental action. A counsellor wishing to become involved in training might consider a course of 'training for trainers' (that is acquiring skills in the field of teaching and learning) and would almost certainly be advantaged by the gaining of a higher degree by research, especially if the aim is to work in higher education. Counsellors who seek accreditation will

Box 8.4 Areas for personal development (after Feltham, personal communication, 1996)

Career	Relationships	Health
Lifestyle	Sexuality	Spirituality
Politics		
Gender	Race	Disability
Class		
Creativity	Fun/Humour	Emotionality
Rationality	Effectiveness	Assertiveness

- What is unresolved?
- What is chronically avoided or put off?
- What are my unhealthy and self-defeating habits?
- What are my constant or repeating anxieties and fears?
- How self-accepting am I?
- How complacent am I?

address developmental plans to filling any gaps in training, practice, supervision and to being able to demonstrate an ongoing commitment to their growth as practitioners. For some counsellors development plans may centre on increased personal resources (see Box 8.4). This may involve entering therapy or a personal growth group but meditation, yoga or similar practices might serve the same ends. Counsellors who feel that their developmental aims would best be served by an increased understanding of the richness and variety of human nature may find that a programme of reading fiction, biography and autobiography contributes substantially. There are as many developmental strategies as there are therapists, but the question that automatically follows on from 'Where do I want to be and what do I want to achieve?' is 'How do I get there from here?'

Constructing a programme for continuing development

When counsellors have reached a decision as to the needs and desires for development and have determined their resources, it remains to design and implement a programme to meet those needs and address those desires. A practical and effective programme should contain both short-term and long-term goals and, in part, it should comprise a 'timetable'. I don't mean that there should be rigid objectives to be achieved on or before a pre-determined date but that there is a sequence to the proposed achievements and an indication of the time by when they might be accomplished. An informed programme of continuing development may have immediate goals, goals to be met in one year, goals to be met in five years and, for the forward-looking or clear-thinking, even goals to be met in ten years. The more clearly stated goals are, the easier it is to formulate a strategy by which they may be achieved and the easier it is to evaluate the programme of continuing development.

A place for any counsellor to start is to sketch out some plan of the order in which developmental objectives may be achieved. Some may take a given period of time; some may be dependent on others being achieved first. Placing aims or goals in time order begins to indicate the steps on the ladder of continuing development and helps to clarify the precise nature of the necessary process. For instance, if an aim is to gain employment as a counsellor in a large organisation (e.g. a college), a survey of job advertisements indicates that preference will be given to accredited counsellors with experience of the client group. This may give rise to the secondary aims of gaining accreditation and relevant experience (for which it may be necessary to work in a voluntary capacity).

For those wishing to become accredited counsellors, the BAC sets out very clearly a number of obligatory preconditions – these may in turn give rise to a number of tertiary aims. For a qualified counsellor in this position, a programme of development now becomes apparent. It might look something like this:

- *Year One*: Satisfy any remaining training, practice and super-vision requirements for accreditation. (For counsellors trained to certificate level this is likely to be a longer process.)
- *Year Two*: Apply for accreditation.
- *Year Three*: Apply for positions of the desired kind.

Of course this programme is over-simplified and to meet the ultimate goal of employment with a large organisation of any kind would almost certainly necessitate other achievements, experience and qualifications but it may serve to illustrate the stepwise nature of continuing development.

Two case illustrations

Longer-term goals are not necessarily deterministic and confining: they may legitimately be about keeping options open. For example, Martin Gill (personal communication, 1996), a newly qualified counsellor working in the National Health Service, was thinking about his future. He said that he had no clear idea of what he wanted it to be. He knew that, when his temporary contract terminated in a year, he wished to continue as a practitioner in the broad area of counselling and psychotherapy. He knew too that although he was well versed in the theory and practice of his chosen orientation (person centred), in his encounters with colleagues who for the most part were informed by psychodynamic theory, he was coming across concepts and language with which he was less familiar. Gill wanted to be able to understand these concepts and to explain his own in a way that his colleagues would understand. Lastly, these encounters had made Gill aware of what seemed to be very different approaches and philosophies with respect to initial contact with clients and potential clients. He wondered whether these differences were really so great and what their implications were for practice and outcome. This was something he really wanted to know more about.

Martin Gill said that he was vague about his development aims. In the course of a relatively short conversation with me, it became apparent that he knew:

- He wanted to enhance his skills as a person centred counsellor and to continue in practice for the foreseeable future.
- He wished to have a greater understanding of psychodynamic theory and practices.
- He had a definite 'research question'.
- He wanted to keep his options open.
- His immediate resources included a limited amount of money but enough time for part-time study.

As a result of this conversation, Gill was in a position to consider how he might satisfy some or all of these developmental desires and he went away to consider the possibility of registering for a higher degree by research which might meet his needs in the following ways:

- It would involve him in reflecting upon his own practice and that of other practitioners, both person centred and psychodynamic.
- The necessary background reading and literature review would include what amounted to a programme of self-instruction in the language and concepts of the psychodynamic approach. This would be augmented by dialogues with psychodynamic practitioners.
- It would provide an opportunity to satisfy his curiosity and perhaps to contribute to the theory and practice of counselling in general.
- A higher degree by research (together with a professional qualification) even at MA level is more versatile (in the sense that it meets any general requirement for a degree or higher degree and may open additional doors because it implies subject knowledge *and* the ability to conduct research) than a taught MA. This versatility might pave the way to a number of employment opportunities, a flexibility desirable in view of Gill's uncertainty about his future plans.
- He could afford to register as a part-time student and could allocate sufficient time to his study.

Upon reflection, Martin Gill decided that to register for a higher degree by research would meet many of his developmental objectives for the next one to two years, and he embarked on such a course of study.

Developmental objectives may be much more precise than Martin Gill at first believed his to be. In my own case while working as a practitioner/manager in a social service mental health facility, I became acutely aware of a personal need for development. This centred on my awareness that I wished to enhance my skills as a practitioner and that I had a desire to study for its own sake. At the same time, I was increasingly aware of my wish to include a larger element of training in the work that I did. Two career ambitions became apparent. These were:

- to embark on a further course of training for myself, preferably one that would allow me to find out about something novel and interesting and which would lead to a qualification;
- to work at least some of the time as a trainer.

A closer examination of my first aim revealed to me that I quite specifically wanted to work with a specific trainer (Jenny Biancardi) whose approach I particularly admired and whose knowledge and expertise I appreciated. At the time Jenny offered training in group work, counselling and psychodrama. I was already a qualified counsellor and considered myself to be an experienced group worker; my experience of psychodrama indicated that it was exciting and powerful and it certainly had novelty value for me. I decided to train as a psychodramatist. To qualify I projected as likely to take me four years.

To meet my second aim of offering my skills as a trainer, I thought about ways in which I could prove my worth and improve my skills. With a colleague and relying upon my experience as a counsellor and training sessions I had conducted with my own staff, I approached the training section of the department for which I worked, offering short courses in counselling skills. My offer was accepted and the courses were successful.

'Scratching the itch' of these easily recognised (and quite imperative) developmental needs has had remarkable consequences. After my projected four years, I did become qualified as a psychodramatist and so a registered psychotherapist (not an original aim but very useful nonetheless). More importantly, if less publicly, I achieved my goal of learning a lot from Jenny Biancardi. My psychodrama training and my acquaintance with Jenny led me to formulate other aims to do with my understanding and practice of the person centred approach (which I am still in the process of achieving) and I became a member of the executive committee of the British Psychodrama Association and the editor of its journal. Similarly, my experience as a trainer convinced me that my heart's desire lay in that direction. This led me to formulate goals which eventually resulted in my appointment to my present post as a lecturer.

The process of review

Reviewing a programme of professional and personal development includes monitoring and evaluation (which I wrote about in Chapter 1) and taking a further step. Monitoring and evaluating are (respectively) ways of providing answers to the questions in Box 8.5.

Box 8.5   Questions for monitoring and evaluation

- How is my programme doing so far?
- Is it still relevant to my needs?
- Have my personal or professional circumstances changed in ways that make this development redundant?

and

- In terms of my original aims and any subsequent reformulation of those aims, how effective (or satisfying, rewarding, valuable, etc.) has my programme been?

To complete the process of review, it is necessary to ask the further question:

- Where do I go from here (what, as a result of this programme do I now want or need to do)?

Reviewing a programme of development (however formal or informal that programme might be) embraces a forward-looking element. In the example of my own development above, it was through the process of review that I decided that I wished to work in the area of counsellor/therapist training. An evaluation of my experiences as a trainer and my keen awareness of my perpetual curiosity were very clear indicators of my desire for a career which combined practice, training and research.

Providing evidence of successful development

For individual counsellors who engage in continuing development for their own satisfaction, subjective or introspective evidence available from formal or informal review may be sufficient. If the intention is to satisfy the requirements of a professional association (particularly for accreditation or registration) a more objective or structured approach to the provision of evidence may be necessary. Where professional bodies specify requirements for continuing development, these requirements tend to be for quantity (e.g. so many days a year). Sufficient evidence to indicate that such a requirement has been met would include a diary recording events attended or projects completed and/or certificates of attendance from the organisers of workshops, seminars and conferences.

The professional bodies (whatever the requirements specified in codes of ethics and practice or for accreditation/re-accreditation) are more likely to be impressed by evidence which supports a statement of what has been learned from or what is different about a counsellor as a result of engaging in continuing development. This is likely too to be more personally satisfying to the practitioner than a simple log of lectures heard or therapy sessions attended. Evidence of this nature may be essentially subjective (although concrete evidence like the provision of a new course, publication of an article or an expanded practice role may be available) and may have to be taken on trust but it is well worth the effort it takes to put together.

To collate and collect evidence of successful development it makes most sense to start with the aims of that development. The clearer the initial statement about needs and desires, the easier it will be to show how they were met and what was achieved. If these aims can be dated and their relevance to the practitioner indicated, so much the better. Stages in the development process can be recorded in a 'portfolio'. This is more than a diary of events. It comprises a record (preferably a contemporary record) of what was done, what happened (and may include some documentary evidence) *and* an indication of the thoughts and feelings of the counsellor making the record. In other words, it includes the reflections and estimations of the practitioner. These may be reflections on the value of a particular event, reflections about personal learning, a re-evaluation of development needs, estimations of the effectiveness of new learning (e.g. any change in attitudes to or practices with clients) and so on. Any objective evidence (e.g. a copies of letters, certificates of attendance) also belong in this portfolio as do the results of any monitoring process incorporated into the programme. It may be worth considering how to make use of the observations of other people with respect to the continuing development of the counsellor. Would a statement from a supervisor, colleague or manager be useful? Lastly, the portfolio is a place to record the evaluation of personal and professional development.

A portfolio indicating continuing development may be highly personal and is likely to be too lengthy for appraisers, accreditors and prospective employers to consider in its entirety. For these (and perhaps other) reasons it may be worth preparing a synopsis of the portfolio, parts of which can then be offered in support.

Box 8.6   Questions leading to evidence of development

1. What were my aims? What did I want to be different?
2. Why did I have these aims?
3. What have I done to meet these aims?
4. What are my reflections on this process?
5. How (if at all) have my thoughts and aims changed during the process of development?
6. What objective or external evidence of my achievements can I offer?
7. What has been useful, constructive and helpful?
8. What has been less useful or disappointing?
9. What new development needs have come to light?
10. Which of the original aims have been achieved?
11. Which have fallen by the wayside? If any, was it because they seemed irrelevant, were superseded or too difficult to achieve?
12. Where do I go from here and why?
13. How have I changed and how has this influenced my work?

Such a synopsis need only be a side or two of A4 paper in length and could result from working to the headings in Box 8.6.

Professional and personal development can be enjoyable and constructive if it is about counsellors working to their own agenda. Thinking constructively about desired changes and achievements and formulating a strategy or a plan (however informal) is a helpful way to make the process fruitful. Monitoring, evaluation and the collection and collation of evidence enrich this, for they facilitate a sense of achievement and provide an opportunity to think about needs and desires in a productive way.

Summary

Appropriate programmes of development are linked to the specific needs of the individual practitioner and change with time. Counsellors may design, implement and review a personally relevant programme.

Programmes of development are limited by available resources. These include those of money, time and restricted access. These limitations should be considered in the first instance.

Developmental needs arise from external circumstances (for example demands of the workplace), professional curiosity, personal needs for growth or therapy and ambition. These needs may be prioritised. Some developmental needs relate to current work, others to the future.

When the developmental needs and desires are known and resources determined, it remains to design and implement a programme to satisfy those needs and desires. A programme of clearly stated goals and a realistic timetable is most likely to result in satisfactory development.

The process of review (including monitoring and evaluation) is important to professional and personal development. Review provides not only an opportunity to look back but also to look forward and determine new needs.

Professional bodies may expect evidence of continuing development. Where these associations specify a requirement, it is likely to be for quantity. A record of events attended, projects completed perhaps with (for example) certificates of attendance may be satisfactory. The quality of development is likely to be viewed as more important than its quantity.

The more clearly aims have been stated, the easier it will be to demonstrate that they have been met. Stages in the developmental process may be recorded in a portfolio which may comprise professional logs, extracts from personal logs and more 'objective' evidence. For purposes of accreditation, it may be advisable to prepare a synopsis of this portfolio.

Appendix: Personal and Professional Development on a Budget

Many counsellors and other therapists find that the availability of time and money limits their opportunities for continuing development. Attendance at a conference will perhaps cost hundreds of pounds, a course leading to another qualification thousands. Added to these costs (for those in private practice) must be added the loss of income from any time taken off work. Even those employed by institutions or agencies may find that they must take annual leave to meet their commitment to professional and personal development. Personal therapy (and perhaps supervision) may make further inroads on the pocket and may have to be outside the normal working day, thus cutting into time for self, family and friends. The obligations of counsellors to their clients, the commitment to professional organisations and personal desires to increase skills and abilities make continuing development a necessity. I am not suggesting that such development should be cost-free or effortless but I do think it reasonable to ask how might a counsellor with a restricted budget achieve this?

Personal and professional development is not necessarily expensive. Throughout this book, I have pointed out cheap but effective ways of meeting the requirements for continuing development. These are summarised below.

Training

With respect to training (i.e. the acquisition of knowledge and skills) the choice is between formal education leading to a qualification, short courses (e.g. weekends, training conferences, summer schools) and a programme of self-teaching.

Courses of formal training tend to be expensive but quality isn't necessarily a function of price. Part-time study is often cheaper than full-time study and courses which include an element of distance learning may be cheaper still. Not all institutions charge the same for similar courses. It may be worth shopping around. Costs in the public sector may be lower than those in the private sector. Higher degrees by research may be cheaper than taught higher degrees and may offer greater flexibility. Some institutions and professional bodies offer financial assistance to would-be counsellors who are struggling to meet the costs of their training and professional development loans are available from some banks. If you meet the conditions, it is probably worth applying for such assistance. Although it doesn't reduce the cost, some institutions accept payment for courses in instalments.

Short courses and workshops vary greatly in cost, fees for a day workshop ranging from £25 to £200. Those provided by local groups tend to be cheaper than those at a national level and may even be free to members (sometimes the cost of membership is less than the price of a single workshop). Some professional organisations (e.g. the BAC) offer bursaries to enable impecunious counsellors to attend the annual training conference. Even 'star' names may be available at the lower price range if you shop around. Combining your resources with those of friends and colleagues may enable you to 'buy in' a specific workshop or specialist for a day or longer.

Determining and implementing a programme of study for yourself is the cheapest alternative but it does have drawbacks. It is harder to offer an 'objective' assessment of what has been learned – a training course leads to a qualification; short programmes may offer certificates of attendance. Without the support of tutors, workshop leaders and colleagues it is also more difficult for the student to be sure of what has been assimilated. Some people may also find the absence of the discipline of a taught course a problem. With all these drawbacks, this form of 'home study' offers a valuable and viable way of increasing knowledge and, if the reading material is chosen wisely, it may be as valid as more formal input.

Personal therapy

Hour for hour, therapy often costs even more than training. Qualified therapists in private practice and in good standing charge on average somewhere between £20 and £40 for a session. A session may be an hour but is just as likely to be 50 (or even 45) minutes. One-to-one therapy may be exactly what is required, in which case there are few alternatives to choosing the 'right' therapist and paying the price. Such alternatives as there are may meet only short-term needs, e.g. the services provided in primary health care, or may mean availing oneself of the services of a less experienced counsellor or therapist. Trainees sometimes offer therapy at a reduced rate because of their status and because they need the practice. This is a mutually convenient relationship in which the counselling may be just as good as that available from many qualified practitioners.

Some needs for therapy may be just as well (or better) met in group therapy. In terms of unit time, this is cheaper than one-to-one therapy and, because it involves interactions with and feedback from fellow group members, it may be more appropriate.

Lastly, it may be possible to find 'free' therapy. Practitioners engaged in research sometimes offer their services free in return for collaboration in their research. Precisely what this means will vary with the practitioner and the research, and perhaps such opportunities are not common but they do exist. Some therapists offer a barter system, exchanging counselling sessions for goods or services as part of a pool of workers.

Supervision

The developmental aspects of supervision may be even better addressed in group supervision than in one-to-one supervision. As with group therapy, this is cheaper. Supervisors-in-training, because they need the practice, may offer supervision more cheaply but may be more interested in functions of supervision other than those of development.

Self-supervision is a way for practitioners to reflect on their own working and all of us can benefit from developing a healthy 'internal supervisor' (see Casement, 1985: 29–56).

Contributing to the furtherance of knowledge

Writing, research, the presentation of knowledge in the form of workshops, seminars, spoken papers, etc. don't necessarily have any monetary cost. All of these take time (and sometimes a lot of it) and the loss of this time may mean a reduction in income but not expenditure. These are ideal ways of engaging in continuing development for practitioners who are swayed to the 'academic' or to communicating their experience but whose cash resources are restricted.

Resourcing yourself

For counsellors, resourcing the self is essential. It is to do with revitalising and refreshing the spirit, the body and the mind. This can be costly (a week on a health farm could constitute development of this kind but wouldn't be cheap) but it need not be. Activities like yoga which address mind and body together are often offered as 'adult education' as well as by specialist organisations, reading is free if the books are borrowed, relaxation can be a private, solitary affair as well as taking place in a group. These aspects of development cost as much or as little as the practitioner wishes.

References

Ashley, A. (1995) 'Counselling and psychotherapy: is there a difference? A response', *Counselling*, 6 (2): 106.

Aveline, M. (1990) 'The training and supervision of individual therapists', in W. Dryden (ed.), *Individual Therapy: A Handbook*. Milton Keynes: Open University Press.

Aveline, M. and Dryden, W. (eds) (1988) *Group Therapy in Britain*. Milton Keynes: Open University Press.

BAC (1993) *Code of Ethics and Practice for Counsellors*. Rugby: British Association for Counselling.

Bettelheim, B. (1976) *The Uses of Enchantment*. London: Thames & Hudson.

Bloch, S. (1988) 'Research in group psychotherapy', in M. Aveline and W. Dryden (eds), *Group Therapy in Britain*. Milton Keynes: Open University Press.

Bolton, G. (1995) '"Taking the thinking out of it": writing – a therapeutic space', *Counselling*, 6 (3): 215–217.

Bond, T. (1993) *Standards and Ethics for Counselling in Action*. London: Sage.

Brady, J.L., Healy, F.C., Norcross, J.C. and Guy, J.D. (1995) 'Stress in counsellors: an integrative research review', in W. Dryden (ed.), *Stresses of Counselling in Action*. London: Sage.

Burns, D.D. (1989) *Feeling Good Handbook: Using the New Mood Therapy in Everyday Life*. New York: Plume.

Casement, P. (1985) *On Learning from the Patient*. London: Routledge.

Chaplin, J. (1988) *Feminist Counselling in Action*. London: Sage.

Clarkson, P. and Gilbert, M. (1991) 'The training of counsellor trainers and supervisors', in W. Dryden and B. Thorne (eds), *Training and Supervision for Counselling in Action*. London: Sage.

Corey, G. (1994) *Group Counselling*, 4th edn. Pacific Grove, CA: Brooks/Cole.

Daines, B., Gask, L. and Usherwood, T. (1996) *Medical and Psychiatric Issues for Counsellors*. London: Sage.

Dryden, W. (ed.) (1995) *The Stresses of Counselling in Action*. London: Sage.

Dryden, W. and Feltham, C. (1994a) *Developing the Practice of Counselling*. London: Sage.

Dryden, W. and Feltham, C. (1994b) *Developing Counsellor Training*. London: Sage.

Dryden, W. and Palmer, S. (eds) (1994) 'Symposium: stress management and counselling', *British Journal of Guidance and Counselling*, 22 (1): 5–81.

Dufeu, B. (1994) *Teaching Myself*. Oxford: Oxford University Press.

Dupont-Joshua, A. (1994) 'Inter-cultural therapy', *Counselling*, 5 (3): 203–205.

Dupont-Joshua, A. (1995) 'In the counsellor's chair: an interview with Lennox Thomas', *Counselling*, 6 (3): 180–182.

Ernst, S. and Goodison, L. (1981) *In Our Own Hands: A Book of Self-Help Therapy*. London: The Women's Press.

Evison, R. and Horobin, R. (1988) 'Co-counselling', in J. Rowan and W. Dryden (eds), *Innovative Therapy in Britain*. Milton Keynes: Open University Press.

Feltham, C. and Dryden, W. (1994) *Developing Counsellor Supervision*. London: Sage.

Ferrucci, P. (1982) *What We May Be*. Wellingborough, Northants: Thorsons.

Foskett, J. (1994) 'Whither are we led and by whom? A reaction to "Ménage à Trois"', *Counselling*, 5 (2): 137–139.

Frankland, A. (1995) 'An invitation to accreditation – steps towards an emerging profession', *Counselling*, 6 (1): 55–60.

Freud, S. (1937/1964) 'Analysis terminable and interminable', in J. Strachey (ed.), *Complete Psychological Works of Sigmund Freud*. London: Hogarth Press.

Garfield, P.L. (1976) *Creative Dreaming*. London: Futura.

Garfield, S.L. (1980) *Psychotherapy: An Eclectic Approach*. New York: Wiley.

Gendlin, E.T. (1986) *Let Your Body Interpret Your Dreams*. Wilmette, IL: Chiron.

Gibbon, J. (1990) 'Accreditation issues: a personal view', *Counselling*, 1 (2): 39.

Gilbert, P., Hughes, W. and Dryden, W. (1989) 'The therapist as a crucial variable in psychotherapy', in W. Dryden and L. Spurling (eds), *On Becoming a Psychotherapist*. London: Routledge.

Goldberg, C. (1992) *The Seasoned Psychotherapist*. New York: Norton.

Gopelrud, E.N. (1980) 'Social support and stress during the first year of graduate school', *Professional Psychology*, 11: 283–290.

Guy, J. D. (1987) *The Personal Life of the Psychotherapist*. New York: Wiley.

Hawkins, P. and Shohet, R. (1989) *Supervision in the Helping Professions*. Milton Keynes: Open University Press.

Hicks, C. and Wheeler, S. (1994) 'Research: an essential foundation for counselling, training and practice', *Counselling*, 5 (1): 29–31.

Jacobs, M. (1988) *Psychodynamic Counselling in Action*. London: Sage.

James, I. (1995a) 'What is CPD about? Continuing professional development and counselling psychology', *Counselling Psychology Review*, 10 (1): 7–9.

James, I. (1995b) 'BPS continuing professional development "recommended" status: would you like to advertise using it?', *Counselling Psychology Review*, 10 (1): 5–6.

Jenkins, P. (1992) 'Counselling and the law', *Counselling*, 3 (3): 165–167.

Jenkins, P. (1993) 'Counselling and the Children Act 1989', *Counselling*, 4 (4): 274–276.

Jenkins, P. (1995) 'Two models of counselling training: becoming a person or learning to be a skilled helper', *Counselling*, 6 (3): 203–206.

Jenkins, P. (1996) *Counselling, Psychotherapy and the Law*. London: Sage.

Jung, C. (1966) 'Psychology of the transference', in *The Practice of Psychotherapy* (Volume 16, Bollingen Series). Princeton, NJ: Princeton University Press.

Kagan, N. (1984) 'Interpersonal process recall: basic methods and recent research', in D. Larsen (ed.), *Teaching Psychological Skills*. Monterey, CA: Brooks/Cole.

Kagan, N., Kratwohl, D.R. and Miller, R. (1963) 'Stimulated recall in therapy using videotape – a case study', *Journal of Counseling Psychology*, 10: 237–243.

Karp, M. (1989) 'Living vs. survival: a psychotherapist's journey', in W. Dryden and L. Spurling (eds), *On Becoming a Psychotherapist*. London: Routledge.

Karp, M. (1991) 'It only hurts when you can't laugh', *Bulletin of the British Psychodrama Association*. July: 3–10.

Kellerman, P.F. (1992) *Focus on Psychodrama: The Therapeutic Aspects of Psychodrama*. London: Jessica Kingsley.

Kierr, S. (1995) 'Treating anxiety: four case examples', in F.J. Levy (ed.), *Dance and Other Expressive Art Therapies*. London: Routledge.

Kingsland, K. and Kingsland, V. (1976) *Complete Hatha Yoga*. Newton Abbot, Devon: David & Charles.

Knights, B. (1995) *The Listening Reader: Fiction and Poetry for Counsellors and Psychotherapists*. London: Jessica Kingsley.

Kottler, J.A. (1986) *On Being a Therapist*. San Francisco: Jossey-Bass.

Lago, C. (1995) 'BAC Reference Library selected references on counselling practice: counselling culture and race', *Counselling*, 6 (1): 31–32.

Lago, C. and Thompson, J. (1989) 'Counselling and race', in W. Dryden, D. Charles-Edwards and R. Woolfe (eds), *Handbook of Counselling in Britain*. London: Routledge.

Lambers, E. (1992) 'Counselling accreditation', *Counselling*, 3 (2): 81–82.

Lockley, P. (1995) *Counselling Heroin and Other Drug Users*. London: Free Association Books.

Lynch, G. (1996) 'What is truth? A philosophical introduction to counselling research', *Counselling*, 7 (2): 144–148.

McCormick, E.W. (1996) *Change for the Better: Life-enhancing Self Help Psychotherapy Approach*, 2nd edn. London: Cassell.

McLeod, J. (1993) *An Introduction to Counselling*. Buckingham: Open University Press.

McLeod, J. (1994) *Doing Counselling Research*. London: Sage.

McLeod, J. (1995) 'Evaluating the effectiveness of counselling: what we don't know', *Changes*, 13 (3): 198–199.

Mahrer, A. (1971) 'Personal life change through systematic use of dreams', *Psychotherapy: Theory, Research and Practice*, 8 (4): 328–332.

Martin, T., Foskett, J., Russell, G. and Potter, J. (1992) 'Angels, fools and lovers', *Counselling*, 3 (2): 86.

Masson, J. (1992) *Against Therapy*. London: Fontana.

Mearns, D. (1994) *Developing Person Centred Counselling*. London: Sage.

Merry, T. (1994) 'Editorial', *Person Centred Practice*, 2(2).

Mowbray, R. (1995) *The Case against Psychotherapy Registration: A Conservation Issue for the Human Potential Movement*. London: Trans Marginal Press.

Naylor-Smith, A. (1994) 'Counselling and psychotherapy: is there a difference?', *Counselling*, 5 (4): 284–287.

Norcross, J.C. and Guy, J.D. (1989) 'Ten therapists: the process of becoming and being', in W. Dryden and L. Spurling (eds), *On Becoming a Psychotherapist*. London: Routledge.

Norcross, J.C. and Prochaska, J.O. (1986) 'Psychotherapist heal thyself – I. The psychological distress and self-change of psychologists, counselors, and lay persons', *Psychotherapy*, 23: 102–114.

Orlans, V. (1993) 'The counsellor's life crisis', in W. Dryden (ed.), *Questions and Answers on Counselling in Action*. London: Sage.

Orlinsky, D.E. and Howard, K.I. (1978) 'The relation of process to outcome in psychotherapy', in S.L. Garfield and A.E. Bergin (eds), *Handbook of Psychotherapy and Behaviour Change: An Empirical Analysis*, 2nd edn. New York: Wiley.

Page, S. and Wosket, V. (1994) *Supervising the Counsellor: A Cyclical Model*. London: Routledge.

Palmer, S. (1991) 'Continuing professional education and supervision', *Counselling*, 2 (4): 122.

Palmer, S. (1995a) 'In the supervisor's chair: Stephen Palmer interviews Brenda Clowes, BAC recognised supervisor', *Counselling*, 6 (1): 28–30.

Palmer, S. (1995b) 'The stresses of running a stress management centre', in W. Dryden (ed.), *The Stresses of Counselling in Action*. London: Sage.

Pandelis, S. (1995) 'A chance for therapy without therapy', *Bulletin of the British Psychodrama Association*, January: 9–10.

Parker, M. (1995) 'Practical approaches: case study writing', *Counselling*, 6 (1): 19–21.

Parsons, S. (1995) *Searching for Healing: Making Sense of the Many Paths to Healing*. Oxford: Lion.

Phung, T.-C. (1995) 'An experience of inter-cultural counselling: views from a black client', *Counselling*, 6 (1): 61–62.

Proctor, B. (1994) 'Supervision – competence, confidence, accountability', *British Journal of Guidance and Counselling*, 22 (3): 309–318.

Reason, P. and Rowan, J. (eds) (1981) *Human Inquiry: A Sourcebook of New Paradigm Research*. Chichester: Wiley.

Rogers, C.R. (1961) *On Becoming a Person*. London: Constable.

Rogers, N. (1985) *The Creative Connection: A Person Centred Approach to Expressive Therapy*. Santa Rosa, CA: The Person Centred Expressive Therapy Institute.

Rowan, J. (1976) *Ordinary Ecstasy: Humanistic Psychology in Action*. London: Routledge & Kegan Paul.

Rowan, J. (1983) *The Reality Game: A Guide to Humanistic Counselling and Therapy*. London: Routledge.

Rowan, J. (1989) 'A late developer', in W. Dryden and L. Spurling (eds), *On Becoming a Psychotherapist*. London: Routledge.

Rowan, J. (1993) *Discover Your Subpersonalities: Our Inner World and the People In It*. London: Routledge.

Rowan, J. and Dryden, W. (eds) (1988) *Innovative Therapy in Britain*. Milton Keynes: Open University Press.

Russell, J. and Dexter, G. (1993) '"Ménage à Trois": accreditation, NVQs and BAC', *Counselling*, 4 (4): 266–269.

Satir, V. (1987) 'The therapist's story', in M. Baldwin and V. Satir (eds), *The Use of Self in Therapy*. New York: Haworth Press.

Schon, D.A. (1991) *The Reflective Practitioner: How Professionals Think in Action*. Aldershot: Avebury.

Shipton, G. (1994) 'Swords into ploughshares: working with resistance to research', *Counselling*, 5 (1): 38–40.

Silverstone, L. (1994) 'Person centred art therapy: bringing the person centred approach to the therapeutic use of art', *Person Centred Practice*, 2 (1): 18–23.

Skovholt, T. and Ronnestad, M.H. (1995) *The Evolving Professional Self: Stages and Themes in Therapist and Counselor Development*. Chichester: Wiley.

Stewart, I. and Joines, V. (1987) *TA Today: A New Introduction to Transactional Analysis*. Nottingham: Lifespace.

Stoltenberg, C. and Delworth, U. (1987) *Supervising Counsellors and Therapists: A Developmental Approach*. San Francisco: Jossey-Bass.

Storr, A. (1979) *The Art of Psychotherapy*. London: Secker & Warburg.

Thorne, B. (1992) 'Psychotherapy and counselling: the quest for differences', *Counselling*, 3 (4): 244–248.

Trower, P., Casey, A. and Dryden, W. (1988) *Cognitive-Behavioural Counselling in Action*. London: Sage.

van Deurzen-Smith, E. (1991) '1992 – and all that BAC Conference 1991', *Counselling*, 2 (4): 133–134.

Wilkins, P. (1994) 'Sexual relationships between counsellors and ex-clients: can they ever be right?', *Counselling*, 5 (3): 206–209.

Wilkins, P. (1995) 'A creative therapies model for the group supervision of counsellors', *British Journal of Guidance and Counselling*, 23 (2): 245–257.

Wood, B., Klein, S., Cross, H.J., Lammers, C.J. and Elliot, J.K. (1985) 'Impaired practitioners: psychologists' opinions about prevalence, and proposals for intervention', *Professional Psychology: Research and Practice*, 16: 843–850.

Woolfe, R., Dryden, W. and Charles-Edwards, D. (1989) 'The nature and range of counselling practice', in W. Dryden, D. Charles Edwards and R. Woolfe (eds), *Handbook of Counselling in Britain*. London: Routledge.

Index